CALLWEY

BAR BIBLE

Contents

Foreword by Dushan Zaric

The first time I met Cihan was one evening at our place, "Employees Only" in New York. I had already heard about him before. Of course you pay attention when your bartender buddies tell you that the guy from Munich's "Schumann's Bar" was visiting last night. Cihan turned out to be incredibly nice and respectful, a true master of the European bartender tradition. Someone who naturally has tons of charisma, but is way too tactful and humble to show it off. Someone who makes the people lucky enough to call him a friend (myself included) feel truly blessed.

When we met that night, we both had a ton of questions. I wanted to know everything about "Schumann's," and he grilled me about "EO." Back then, we became friends; he and some of his bartender buddies kept coming back to New York, and our bar team made return visits to "Schumann's." We basically became brother and sister bars. On one of those visits, they asked me to guest bartend at "Schumann's." I was super curious and honestly felt honored that they let me behind the bar; after all, I knew how precise they worked and how much they had to do. That night, I was behind the bar with Cihan and his team. I was seriously impressed by how smoothly the service ran: orders were taken non-stop, drinks were whipped up, and food was served without a break. I watched Cihan make his cocktails while casually chatting with several guests sitting at the bar. At "Schumann's," they used the free pouring technique, where the drink is poured in a long stream from the bottle into the glass—without the usual pour spout. And without a measuring cup, too. And every bartender did their job with a real sense of humility and genuine curiosity. That impressed me endlessly.

Back then, Cihan already had a big influence in the industry, he was a consultant and shared his expertise with people all over the world. He's part of the new generation of German and European bartenders who not only mix flawless cocktails, but also remind us that class and humility are key elements of real hospitality. At his bar "Circle" in Munich, Cihan took contemporary and classic cocktails to perfection and gave his guests unforgettable experiences.

I'm sure both cocktail fans and pro bartenders will appreciate his cocktail book just as much. Cihan's unique mixing techniques and his attitude turn even the simplest creations into liquid treasures. I can't wait to get my hands on my copy and finally try out some of his fascinating creations myself.

DUSHAN ZARIĆ
Co-founder "Employees Only NYC"
www.employeesonlynyc.com

Foreword by Alex Kratena

It was a typical Tuesday or Wednesday night—so normal that I can't even remember which day it was. The bar was busy, but nothing surprising was happening. When things calmed down, I went to the back to have a coffee and check my emails.

While I was sitting there with my espresso, I read a message offering me a guest bartender gig in Germany. I could hardly believe my eyes: it was about "Schumann's"—wow!

I'd met Cihan a few times before; but now we were going to be behind the bar together for the first time. When I arrived, he greeted me right away. He showed me around, introduced me to everyone on the team—everything under control, everything ready—and then took me out to eat.

The next day, while we were getting ready and I was having a quick coffee, Cihan disappeared for a moment into the staff room. He came back, handed me a tie and a jacket, and said: You're wearing this tonight.

I couldn't believe it—the guys had a jacket made for my shift and even had my name embroidered on it. The place was buzzing that night, loads of people showed up, and of course I was struggling, since I'd never worked there before and was having a hard time finding my way around. But every time I looked to my right, Cihan was there, and instead of freaking out, he just radiated endless positive energy.

A few years later, I was back in town and since Cihan knew I was coming, he insisted on picking me up. When I walked through the glass doors at the airport, there he was, beaming, in a great mood and incredibly kind, even though it was late and he'd just finished work. He'd changed his schedule and drove all the way to the airport just to have coffee with me, chat, and take me into the city. We went to the parking garage, and I was impressed: the guy drove an absolutely fantastic car. In London I always ride my bike, so I just couldn't resist making a comment.

But Cihan wasn't trying to show off his cool car, he just wanted to have a coffee and chat with me. He said he gets a different car every few months because he's a brand ambassador.

Last year I taught several classes in Germany and needed a venue. So who do I call? Of course, Cihan! I knew he wanted to open a new bar, and I was dying to check it out. When I walked into the place, I was fascinated—not just by the concept, the drinks, and the stylish setup, but especially by all the tiny details this guy had thought of. I definitely stole a few of my ideas from there.

That evening we held our event at the bar, and while having coffee, Cihan showed me the drinks menu. Normally, there were simple drink menus with five drinks on the tables, but for this night he went all out and hired a local artist to create an amazing three-dimensional pop-up menu. Cihan represents a new generation of modern bartenders. He started small, always worked hard, and never gave up on his dreams. Nothing and no one can stop him from always doing a little more than people expect. He showed everyone that with positive energy, real passion, and contagious enthusiasm, you might not change the world, but you can make your own life richer and brighten the days of the people around you. Those are exactly the qualities that make a great bartender.

If Cihan offers you a drink, a glass of water, or a cup of coffee next time, say yes—there's aways some little extra that'll put a smile on your face.

ALEX KRATENA
Founder
www.alexkratena.com
www.pourdrink.org

CIHAN ANADOLOGLU
MY JOURNEY INTO BAR CULTURE

For me as a bartender, my job is about far more than just serving drinks: I want to create places where people meet and get creative together. Exclusivity and privacy are just as important as quality and a certain amount of playful freedom. In my philosophy, all these elements come together in a unique mix—always with the goal of giving my guests an experience they'll remember.

As a bartender, I'm a craftsman: I create and garnish my cocktails and reinvent myself every single day. That's exactly where my passion lies—always searching for new flavors, textures, and stories in a glass. In my own bar, "Circle by Cihan Anadologlu," I was finally able to really put this philosophy into practice and surprise my guests with unique cocktail creations. From my personal story to the development of the bar and selected recipes, there's always just one thing for me: It's cocktail time!

CIHAN ANADOLOGLU

My passion? Bartending! I took my very first steps into the bar world back in my youth in New York City. After some successful years at the best culinary and hospitality schools in the world, it was time to jump into the working world and learn even more "on the job."

Soon, the highlights of my career followed, like my time as head bartender at the world-famous "Schumann's Bar" in Munich or working with selected Michelin-starred chefs, who always inspired me with new ideas. As an expert in my field, I've opened loads of bars and restaurants all over the globe, living in cities like New York, Hong Kong, London, and Munich. I also do some journalism for different newspapers and magazines.

By now, I'm an internationally renowned bartender, consultant for the food and beverage industry, and an author. With my bar "Circle by Cihan Anadologlu" in Munich, I wrote an important chapter that's now part of my story. I regularly share my know-how as a guest bartender all over the world.

One of my biggest achievements is the "Bacardi Grey Goose Global Finals" award. I had the honor of creating my own cocktail for the Oscars 2014. In 2014, I got another award as bar manager at "Tales of the Cocktail" in New Orleans: "Best International High Volume Cocktail Bar."

Finally, I was able to make my dream come true: With "Circle by Cihan Anadologlu," a bar was born that became my creative center for a while—a place where I brought my vision of drinks and hospitality to life. The "Circle" bar was created on the first floor as a collaboration.

MY JOURNEY WITH CIRCLE

In 2016, I was able to fulfill a big dream: opening my own bar, "Circle by Cihan Anadologlu," in Munich. For me, it was a place where exclusivity met inspiration, where people came together and could experience my idea of bar culture.

The "Circle" was shaped by a Japanese-inspired design, which became a real highlight of the Munich bar scene. It was especially important to me to develop my own essences and liqueurs and put together a spirits selection that was truly one of a kind. The cocktail menu was based on the four seasons—a concept that brought nature into the glass and made every visit a new experience.

"It rarely leaves a good impression on the hosts when a guest suddenly collapses unconscious on the floor."
Anthony Bourdain

The recognition came quickly: "Circle" won the Fizzz Award as "Most Innovative Bar," was listed in Drinks International's "World's Top 100 Cocktail Bars," and was nominated several times at the 2017 Mixology Bar Awards—as "Best European Bar" and "New Bar of the Year."

But for me personally, "Circle" was way more than just a bar. It was a creative lab, a space where I could really put my ideas into action and sharpen my own style. A chapter of my career that's finished now, but still shapes me to this day.

MY PHILOSOPHY ABOUT BARTENDING

"I'm 91 years old and I still don't know how to make sushi perfectly"—those are the words of an old sushi master in Tokyo. That got me thinking: Humility and modesty are the foundation of a happy life. The love for the job, the drive for perfection, the inner satisfaction when guests leave your bar happy—all that made me want to "live" for my profession.

I don't see my job as just "hospitality" or "night work," even if a lot of people call it that. It's really about the love for making sure every guest goes home happy. Openness and honesty with yourself and your guests are just as much a part of hospitality and the foundation of any success.

So, what do you actually do for a living?

I hear this question a lot. Bartending isn't just mixing cocktails, pouring drinks, or something you did "on the side" during college. "Being a bartender isn't easy, it's not about skill, it's about character," said the late bartender Sasha Petraske, and he really nailed it.

We're not mixologists, even though that term gets thrown around a lot these days; I totally reject that label for our profession! We're not artists either, just because we garnish our cocktails. That would be over the top. No Michelin-star chefs calls themselves artists—they're chefs—and it's exactly the same with us—we're bartenders.

We're craftsmen—that's what describes our job best. We know our regulars and always stay in the background. We know when someone's had enough and make sure it never gets that far. We know what our guests like to drink and can already think ahead about the cocktails and drinks. We're not the stars of the night, and we never should be. In short: We know our guests and always have a feel for them and what they want.

Being a bartender is a unique job, it takes some sacrifices, but the passion you bring to it makes up for that pretty quickly! Every day I learn something new, every day is fresh and full of things happening, and every day I reinvent myself!

CREATIVITY, PERFECTION, CURIOSITY, TRADITION, EXPERIENCE, KNOWLEDGE, PURISM, HUMILITY, SERENITY, SURPRISE, ENTERTAINMENT, PROVOCATION—these are the qualities you'll always find in my work. What else can I say? I just love it!

The former Japanese-style— craft cocktail bar "Circle by Cihan Anadologlu" on the first floor of "Hearthouse."

The History of
the Cocktail

The word "cocktail" appeared for the first time in 1803, in the newspaper *Farmer's Cabinet*. Three years later, the *Balance & Columbian Repository* described that the so-called "Bittered Sling" was the name of a cocktail. In response to a letter, Harry Croswell wrote down the definition of the word: "Cock Tail then, is a stimulating liquor, composed of spirits of any kind, sugar, water and bitters, it is vulgary called a bittered sling."

Now, there are plenty more stories about the word "cocktail" and where it came from …

You probably know the cockfight version, right? Immigrants from Mexico and South America had their roosters fight, dedicated the tail of the losing rooster to the winner, toasted the winner with "on the Cocks Tail," and drank to it. It's possible that the word "cocktail" played a role here too—but that's pretty unlikely. The French word "coquetier" is also believed to be part of the cocktail story: meaning "egg cup," it was a drinking vessel.

In a nutshell, no-one can really claim to know where the cocktail actually started. But according to the latest research and debate among historians, cocktails originally had something to do with horses.

To check a horse's health, people used to stick a ginger-rubbed stick up the horse's butt. The horse would immediately open its mouth and show its teeth, so it could be checked before being sold. "On the Cocks Tail" was the toast when the deal went through and everyone celebrated in fine style. This is the latest, most important, and probably earliest, version of the origin of the term "cocktail"—and historians have proven it before all the other theories. By definition, a cocktail is actually a subgroup of mixed drinks—,like juleps, slings, and toddies. Unfortunately, people still use it as a catch-all term for all mixed drinks.

When the cocktail became famous worldwide in the mid-19th century, the bartender's job got more and more attention and became pretty lucrative thanks to clever entertainment. More and more people started drinking "cocktails," which were originally intended as morning medicine.

In the last 15 years of the 19th century, the bar became a meeting place for everyone. By the way, the word "bar" actually comes from "barrier," which was designed to separate the bartender from the guest. There was no minimum drinking age back then—if you could see over the bar, you could drink. Women weren't allowed to enter the "bar" and were only let in for "entertainment" purposes.

One of the most famous bartenders of his time, and the author of the first cocktail book, was Jerry Thomas. His classic *How to Mix Drinks,—The Bonvivant's Companion* was published in 1862. And explained the different categories of beverage, including the class of cocktails.

More and more bartenders started writing cocktail books, which are extremely hard to find these days, but lay the foundations for our profession. This was the beginning of cocktail history.

The first known cocktail was a mix of barley, tartaric acid, honey, and apple juice, found in a roughly 5,000-year-old clay vessel on the banks of the Tigris between Iran and Iraq.

It didn't always have to be Paris or London: Around 1935, Berlin also had a well-established bar culture, like at the Majestic Hotel.

As more and more spirits were distilled and alcohol was exported all over the world, the classics were invented. The recipes from back then aren't really drinkable, and the measurements had to be researched to even understand the cocktail itself. From the beginning of the 20th century, cocktails got more and more popular, and more people started drinking them.

This led to Prohibition from 1919 to 1933. The 14-year alcohol ban totally changed cocktail and bar culture. "Speakeasy bars" popped up all over the USA—they had a reputation for secrecy and a restrictive door policy. The most famous ones were the "21 Club" in Manhattan and the "Green Mile Club" in Chicago. There were also "bootlegged cocktails," which were carried in flasks under the clothes. Secret distilleries made a fortune making alcohol, but they were constantly busted by the police and the booze was destroyed. One legendary name from back then was Al Capone, who got rich smuggling alcohol. Prohibition ended in 1933, and Franklin D. Roosevelt—the US president at the time—was the first to toast its demise with a cocktail.

Of course, people in Europe kept drinking alcohol during this time, and lots of well-known bartenders came up with more classics. One of the most renowned bartenders was Frank Meier from the Ritz Hotel in Paris, with his classic book *The Artistry of Mixing Drinks*. This was also the birth of tiki cocktails. The *Piña Colada*, the *Zombie*, and the *Mai Tai* took over the bars, and old classics faded into the background. This era was known for colorful juices and liqueur-heavy cocktails. People stopped drinking spirit-based 6 to 8 cl cocktails and drinks. Instead, wild names like *Ladykiller*, *Blue Lagoon*, and so on, started showing up on cocktail and bar menus back then.

It wasn't until the 21st century that cocktails had a comeback, and bartenders from New York and London dug up the "lost" recipes again. Germany also played a big part in promoting bar culture and taking things in a new direction.

The result is well known—not only did spirits companies spot the trend and bring forgotten liquors back to the market, but bartenders also revived and sometimes improved recipes from old books.

More and more kitchen gadgets are now part of bar culture, and even medical technology isn't off limits. Infusions, essences, even distilled spirits, plus bitters and high-quality liqueurs are just some of the things bartenders work with nowadays.

Sous-vide machines, which are mostly used in the kitchen, are now standard equipment in every professional cocktail bar. Fresh juices and high-quality spirits and liqueurs are also part of the basic setup. Bartenders mix these and many other ingredients to perfection, bringing both their own creations and classic recipes to everyone—and with them, their inventors too.

"Knowing lots of cocktails and their history is really important and only helps a bartender."

A typical day at the bar in London's Murray's Club in 1932: The bartenders are neatly dressed in uniform, and the international waitresses each have their own unique outfits. In places like this, today's classics were created and mixed for the guests.

Cocktails, Long Drinks and spirits

AROUND THE CLOCK

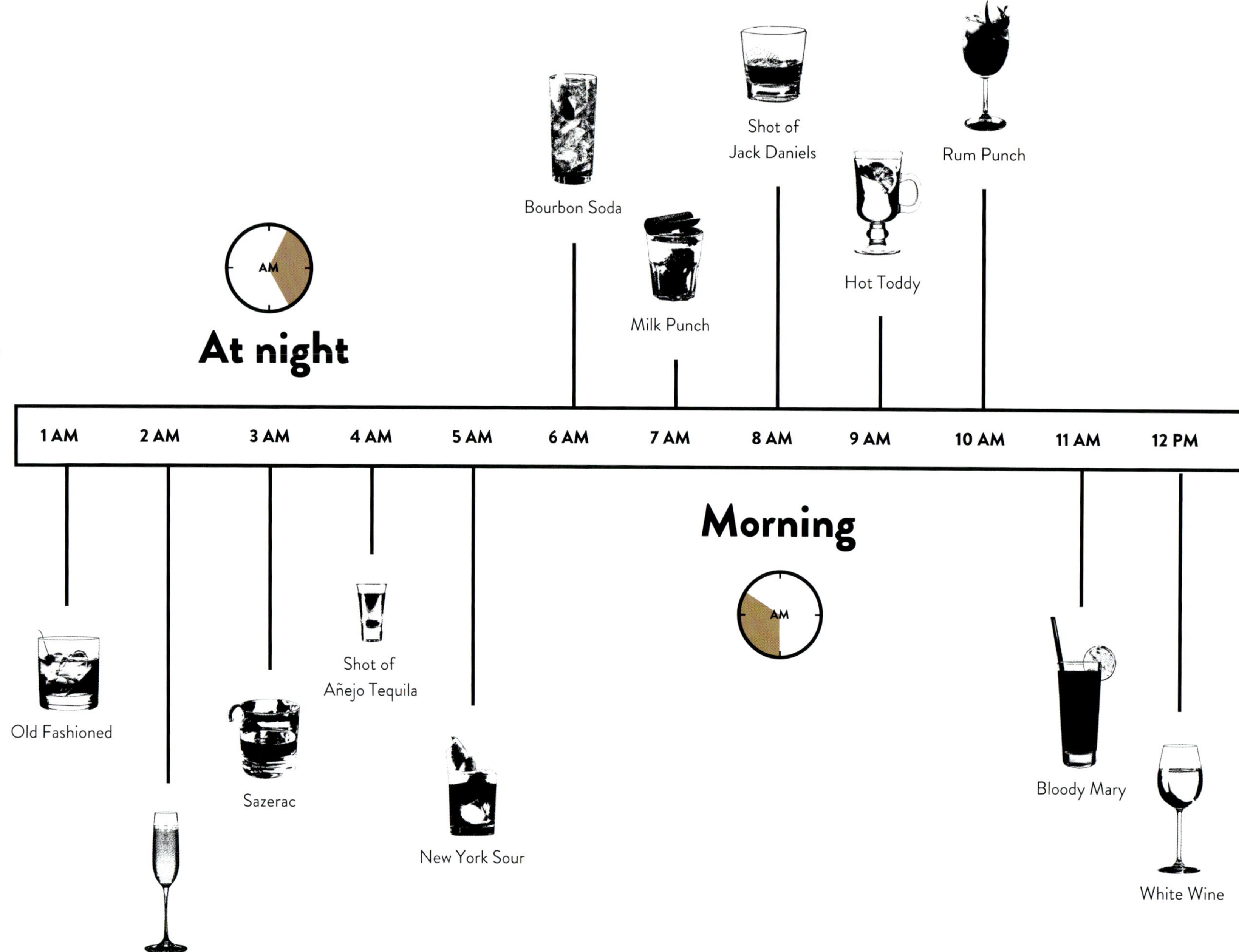

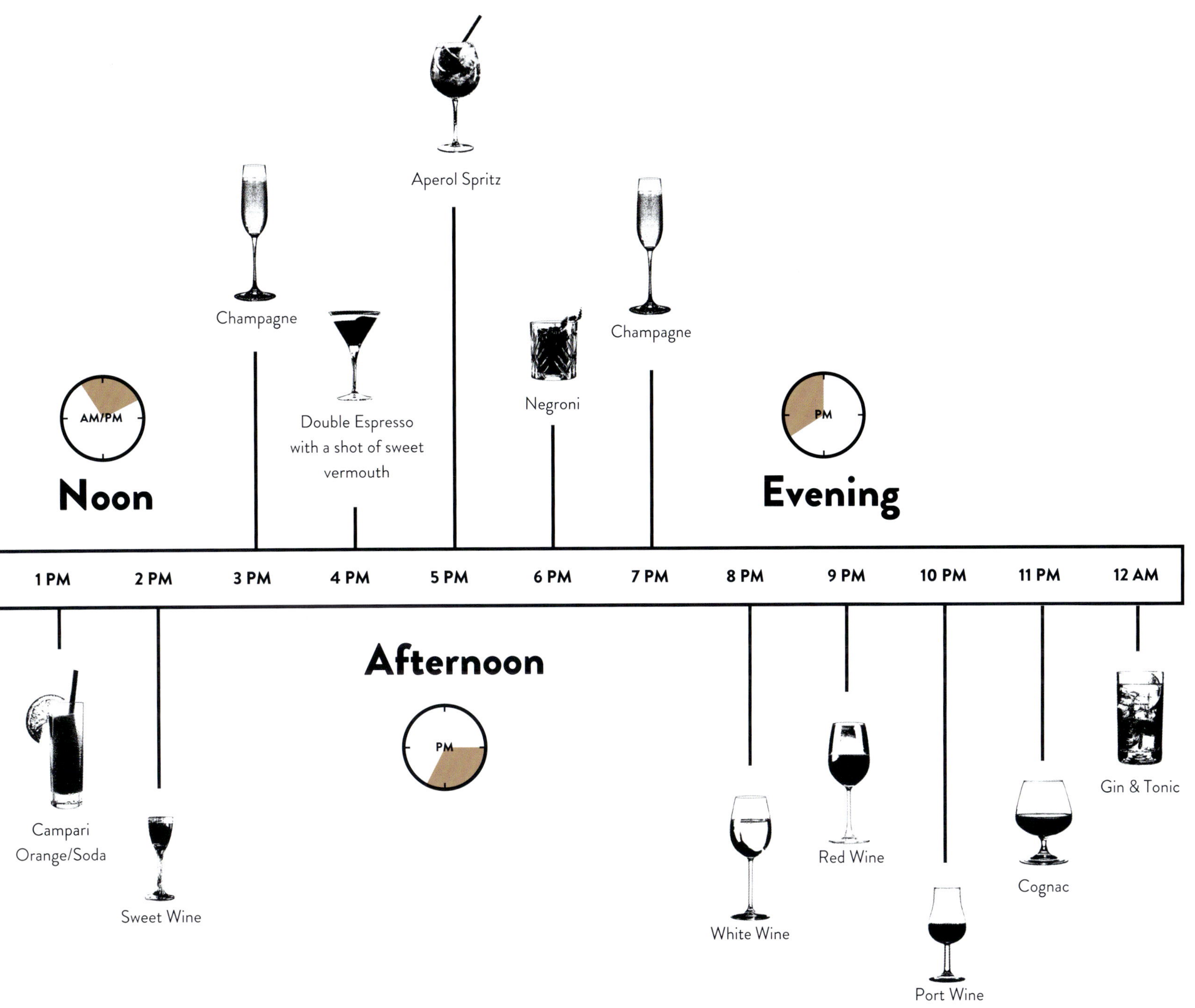
Aperol Spritz
Champagne
Double Espresso
with a shot of sweet
vermouth
Negroni
Champagne
AM/PM
Noon
PM
Evening
1 PM
2 PM
3 PM
4 PM
5 PM
6 PM
7 PM
8 PM
9 PM
10 PM
11 PM
12 AM
Afternoon
PM
Campari
Orange/Soda
Sweet Wine
White Wine
Port Wine
Red Wine
Cognac
Gin & Tonic

The 200 Best Drinks in the World

Classic cocktails are the be-all and end-all of our job. Every bartender or anyone who wants to do this job should know many of these roughly 200 classic recipes, including what's in them, how to make them, and how to garnish them. Of course, there are far more than the 200 classics listed here, but I think we've covered the most important ones that every bartender should know by heart. To help you find the cocktails faster, we've split them up into different spirit groups.

Gin Cocktails

Gin was first mentioned in writing in 1714, in the book *The Fabel of the Bees: or Private Vices, Public Benefits*. For years, it's been the trendiest spirit around and as the main ingredient in loads of cocktails and long drinks, it's a must-have that's not going out of style anytime soon. This fine spirit is usually made from grain or molasses and gets its flavor from juniper and other spices. The king of cocktails is the Martini—originally mixed with genever as a *Martinez Cocktail*, but taken over bar menus everywhere once gin joined the party. Another classic long drink is the Gin & Tonic. A bartender friend of mine once said: "Even if you walk into a bar in jeans and a t-shirt, if you order a Gin & Tonic, you're basically wearing a tux on the inside." We personally love gin and have a great little selection at our place. But we're not just following trends—we try out all sorts of different products. The only thing that really convinces us is the taste.

Alaska

1.4 oz / 4 cl Tanqueray No. TEN Gin
0.3 oz / 1 cl Chartreuse Jaune
1 dash The Bitter Truth Orange Bitters
1 dash amontillado sherry

•

GARNISH
None

•

PREPARATION
Stir gently in a mixing glass over ice for about 10 seconds, then strain into a glass.

•

Glass: cocktail coupe

Alexander

1.0 oz / 3 cl Tanqueray No. TEN Gin
0.7 oz / 2 cl white crème de cacao
1.0 oz / 3 cl cream

•

GARNISH
Nutmeg

•

PREPARATION
Shake well in a shaker over ice for about 10 seconds, then strain into a glass. Grate nutmeg over the finished drink.

Hugo Ensslin, Recipes for Mixed Drinks

Aviation

1.7 oz / 5 cl Tanqueray No. TEN Gin
0.7 oz / 2 cl fresh lemon juice
0.5 oz / 1.5 cl maraschino
1 bs The Bitter Truth Crème de Violette

•

GARNISH
None

•

PREPARATION
Shake well in a shaker over ice for about 10 seconds, then strain into a glass.

•

Glass: cocktail coupe

Hugo Ensslin, Recipes for Mixed Drinks

Bijou

1 oz / 3 cl Tanqueray No. TEN Gin

1 oz / 3 cl Chartreuse Verte
1 oz / 3 cl red vermouth
1 dash The Bitter Truth Orange Bitters

•

GARNISH
None

•

PREPARATION
Stir gently in a mixing glass over ice for about 10
seconds, then strain into a glass.

•

Glass: cocktail coupe

1890

Harry Johnson, Bartenders' Manual

Bramble

↓

2 oz / 6 cl Tanqueray No. TEN Gin
1 oz / 3 cl fresh lemon juice
0.5 oz / 1.5 cl crème de mure (blackberry liqueur)
0.3 oz / 1 cl sugar syrup (see page 222)
4 Blackberries

•

GARNISH
Blackberries
Powdered sugar

•

PREPARATION
Shake vigorously in a shaker over ice for about 10
seconds and strain into the tumbler over crushed
ice. Dust blackberries with powdered sugar and
place them on top.

•

Glass: tumbler

1980s
Years

Dick Bradsell, "Fred's Club Soho," London

Bronx

↓

2 oz / 6 cl Tanqueray No. TEN Gin
0.7 oz / 2 cl dry vermouth
0.7 oz / 2 cl red vermouth
0.7 oz / 2 cl fresh orange juice

•

GARNISH
None

•

PREPARATION
Shake vigorously in a shaker over ice for about
10 seconds and strain into the glass.

•

Glass: cocktail coupe

1908

William Boothby, The World's Drinks and How to mix them

Claridge

↓

1.5 oz / 4.5 cl Tanqueray No. TEN Gin
1.5 oz / 4.5 cl fresh lemon juice
0.5 oz / 1.5 cl orange liqueur or triple sec
0.5 oz / 1.5 cl the Bitter Truth Apricot Brandy

•

GARNISH
Optional: Lemon zest

PREPARATION
Stir gently in a mixing glass over ice for about
10 seconds, then strain into a glass.
Optionally garnish with a lemon twist.

•

Glass: cocktail coupe

1930

Harry Craddock, The Savoy Cocktail Book

Clover Club

↓

2 oz / 6 cl Tanqueray No. TEN Gin
1 oz / 3 cl fresh lemon juice
0.7 oz / 2 cl raspberry syrup
½ egg white

•

GARNISH
Raspberry

•

PREPARATION
Shake vigorously in a shaker over ice for about
10 seconds, strain into a second cup and
shake again for about 10 seconds without ice
("dry shake"). Garnish with a raspberry.

•

Glass: cocktail coupe

1935

Albert Stevens Crockett, The Old Waldorf-Astoria Bar Book

Dirty Martini

↓

2 oz / 6 cl Tanqueray No. TEN Gin
0.3 oz / 1 cl dry vermouth
4 dashes olive brine

•

GARNISH
1 Olive or more (as you like)

•

PREPARATION
Stir gently in a mixing glass over ice for about 10 seconds, then strain into a glass. Garnish with an olive.

•

Glass: martini glass

1933

Franklin D. Roosevelt toasted the end of Prohibition with a Dirty Martini.

Dry Martini Cocktail

↓

2.7 oz / 8 cl Tanqueray No. TEN Gin
0.3 oz / 1 cl Noilly Prat Vermouth

•

GARNISH
1 Medium-sized green olive with pit

•

PREPARATION
Stir gently in a mixing glass over ice for about 10 seconds, then strain into a glass. Add the olive.

Glass: martini glass

c. 1940

Gibson

↓

2 oz / 6 cl Tanqueray No. TEN Gin
0.3 oz / 1 cl dry vermouth

•

GARNISH
1 Cocktail onion or more (as you like)

•

PREPARATION
Stir gently in a mixing glass over ice for about 10 seconds, then strain into a glass. Garnish with a cocktail onion.

•

Glass: martini glass

1908

William Boothby, The World's Drinks and How to Mix Them

Gimlet

↓

1.7 oz / 5 cl Tanqueray No. TEN Gin
1.7 oz / 5 cl Rose's Lime Juice

•

GARNISH
None

•

PREPARATION
Stir gently in a mixing glass over ice for about 10 seconds, then strain into the glass.

Glass: cocktail coupe

1922

Harry MacElhone, Harry's ABC of Mixing Cocktails

Gin & It

↓

2 oz / 6 cl Tanqueray No. TEN Gin
1 oz / 3 cl red vermouth

•

GARNISH
⅛ Orange

•

PREPARATION
Stir gently in a martini glass with ice for about 10 seconds. Squeeze an orange wedge over the drink or drop it in.

•

Glass: martini glass

1890

Used to be served as a Sweet Martini in New York bars.

Gin & Sin

↓

1.4 oz / 4 cl Tanqueray No. TEN Gin
1.4 oz / 4 cl orange juice
0.7 oz / 2 cl lemon juice
0.3 oz / 1 cl sugar syrup (see page 222)
1 dash grenadine

GARNISH

None

•

PREPARATION

Shake in a shaker over ice for about 10 seconds, then strain into the glass.

•

Glass: cocktail coupe

Gin Fizz

2 oz / 6 cl Tanqueray No. TEN Gin

1 oz / 3 cl fresh lemon juice

0.7 oz / 2 cl sugar syrup (see page 222)

2–2.7 oz / 6–8 cl soda water

•

GARNISH

¼ Lemon

•

PREPARATION

Shake in a shaker over ice for about 10 seconds, top up with soda, and strain into the glass. Add a lemon wedge to the finished cocktail.

•

Glass: highball glass

•

VARIATIONS:

Silver Fizz *– with an extra egg white*

Grand Royal Sloe Gin Fizz *– with gin infused with sloes, an extra whole egg, and champagne instead of soda water*

Hanky Panky Cocktail

1.4 oz / 4 cl Tanqueray No. TEN Gin

1.4 oz / 4 cl red vermouth

0.3 oz / 1 cl Fernet Branca

•

GARNISH

None

•

PREPARATION

Stir gently in a mixing glass over ice for about 10 seconds, then strain into a glass.

•

Glass: martini glass

Harry Craddock, The Savoy Cocktail Book

Income Tax Cocktail

1 oz / 3 cl Tanqueray No. TEN Gin

0.7 oz / 2 cl dry vermouth

0.7 oz / 2 cl red vermouth

1 oz / 3 cl fresh orange juice

2 dashes The Bitter Truth Aromatic Bitters

•

GARNISH

Orange zest

PREPARATION

Shake vigorously in a shaker over ice for about 10 seconds, then strain into the glass. Squeeze orange zest over the drink and drop it into the glass.

•

Glass: cocktail coupe

This cocktail was created as an adaptation of the Bronx Cocktail.

Journalist

1.4 oz / 4 cl Tanqueray No. TEN Gin

0.7 oz / 2 cl dry vermouth

0.7 oz / 2 cl red vermouth

0.3 oz / 1 cl lemon juice

0.3 oz / 1 cl triple sec or orange liqueur

2 dashes The Bitter Truth Aromatic Bitters

•

GARNISH

Lemon zest

•

PREPARATION

Stir gently in a mixing glass over ice for about 10 seconds, then strain into a glass. Squeeze lemon zest over the drink and drop it into the glass.

•

Glass: cocktail coupe

Harry Craddock, The Savoy Cocktail Book

Knickerbocker Martini

↓

1.4 oz / 4 cl Tanqueray No. TEN Gin
1 oz / 3 cl dry vermouth
0.3 oz / 1 cl red vermouth

•

GARNISH
Lemon zest

•

PREPARATION
Stir gently in a mixing glass over ice for about 10 seconds, then strain into a glass. Squeeze lemon zest over the drink and drop it into the glass.

•

Glass: martini glass

1930

Harry Craddock, The Savoy Cocktail Book

———

Last Word

↓

0.7 oz / 2 cl Tanqueray No. TEN Gin
0.7 oz / 2 cl Chartreuse Verte
0.7 oz / 2 cl Maraschino
0.7 oz / 2 cl fresh lime juice

•

GARNISH
None

•

PREPARATION
Shake vigorously in a shaker over ice for about 10 seconds and strain into the glass.

Glass: cocktail coupe

1951

Ted Saucier, Bottoms Up

———

Martinez Cocktail

(Grandfather of the Martini cocktail)

↓

1.7 oz / 5 cl Tanqueray No. TEN Gin
1 oz / 3 cl red vermouth
0.3 oz / 1 cl Maraschino
2 dashes The Bitter Truth Orange Bitters

•

GARNISH
Lemon zest

•

PREPARATION
Stir gently in a mixing glass over ice for about 10 seconds, then strain into a glass. Squeeze lemon zest over the drink and drop it into the glass.

•

Glass: martini glass

1884

O.H. Byron, The Modern Bartenders' Guide

———

Martini Cocktail Original

↓

2 oz / 6 cl Tanqueray No. TEN Gin
0.7 oz / 2 cl Noilly Prat Vermouth

2 dashes The Bitter Truth Orange Bitters

•

GARNISH
Lemon zest

•

PREPARATION
Stir gently in a mixing glass over ice for about 10 seconds, then strain into a glass. Squeeze lemon zest over the drink and drop it into the glass.

•

Glass: martini glass

approx. 1888

Probably Harry Johnson, Bartenders' Manual

———

Monkey Gland

↓

2 oz / 6 cl Tanqueray No. TEN Gin
1 oz / 3 cl fresh orange juice
1 dash Pernod or absinthe
2 dashes grenadine

•

GARNISH
Orange zest

•

PREPARATION
Shake well in a shaker over ice for about 10 seconds, then strain into a glass. Squeeze the orange zest over the drink and drop it into the glass.

Glass: cocktail coupe

1920s Years

Harry MacElhone, "Harry's New York Bar," Paris

Negroni

1 oz / 3 cl Tanqueray No. TEN Gin
1 oz / 3 cl Campari
1 oz / 3 cl red vermouth

•

GARNISH
Orange zest

•

PREPARATION
Stir gently in the tumbler for about 10 seconds. Squeeze the orange zest over the drink and drop it into the glass.

•

Glass: tumbler—Old Fashioned glass

1919

"Caffé Casoni," Florence; named after Count Camillo Negroni

Pegu Club

1.7 oz / 5 cl Tanqueray No. TEN Gin
0.3 oz / 1 cl fresh lime juice
0.5 oz / 1.5 cl orange curaçao
1 dash The Bitter Truth Aromatic Bitters
1 dash The Bitter Truth Orange Bitters

•

GARNISH
Orange zest

•

PREPARATION
Shake well in a shaker over ice for about 10 seconds, then strain into a glass. Squeeze the orange zest over the drink and drop it into the glass.

Glass: cocktail coupe

1920

"Pegu Club," Rangoon

Pink Gin

2 oz / 6 cl Tanqueray No. TEN Gin
3 dashes The Bitter Truth Aromatic Bitte

•

GARNISH
Lemon zest

•

PREPARATION
Stir the gin gently over ice in a mixing glass for about 10 seconds. Rinse the martini glass with bitters, then strain in the contents of the mixing glass. Squeeze lemon zest over the drink and drop it into the glass.

•

Glass: martini glass

1824

Dr. Johann Gottlieb Benjamin Siegert, Royal Navy

Pink Lady

2 oz / 6 cl Tanqueray No. TEN Gin
0.3 oz / 1 cl fresh lemon juice
0.3 oz / 1 cl sugar syrup (see page 222)
2 dashes grenadine
1 egg white

GARNISH
None

•

PREPARATION
Shake vigorously in a shaker over ice for about 10 seconds and strain into the glass.

•

Glass: sherry glass

1937

William J. Tarling, Café Royal Cocktail Book

Ramos Gin Fizz

(*also known as* New Orleans Fizz)

2 oz / 6 cl Tanqueray No. TEN Gin
0.5 oz / 1.5 cl fresh lemon juice
0.5 oz / 1.5 cl fresh lime juice
0.7 oz / 2 cl sugar syrup (see page 222)
0.3 oz / 1 cl cream
1 egg white

•

TOPPING
2–2.7 oz / 6–8 cl soda water
6 dashes The Bitter Truth Orange flower Water

•

GARNISH
Lemon zest

•

PREPARATION
Shake vigorously in a shaker over ice for about 10 seconds, top up with soda, and drizzle the foam with orange blossom water. Squeeze lemon zest over the drink and drop it into the glass.

Glass: highball glass

1888

Henry C. Ramos, New Orleans

Red Snapper

↓

2 oz / 6 cl Tanqueray No. TEN Gin
0.3 oz / 1 cl fresh lemon juice
4 oz / 12 cl top-quality tomato juice
6 dashes Worcestershire sauce
2 dashes Tabasco
1 pinch salt
1 pinch black pepper
•

GARNISH
Celery stick
•

PREPARATION
Shake lightly in the shaker for 2 seconds and
strain straight into the highball glass without ice.
Peel the celery stick and put it in the glass.
•

Glass: highball glass

1962

The London Magazine, Vol. 2

Singapore Sling

↓

1.7 oz / 5 cl Tanqueray No. TEN Gin
1 oz / 3 cl fresh lime juice
0.3 oz / 1 cl Cointreau

0.3 oz / 1 cl Bénédictine
0.3 oz / 1 cl grenadine
0.5 oz / 1.5 cl cherry brandy
3.4 oz / 10 cl top-quality pineapple juice
•

GARNISH
Maraschino cherry (best if soaked in
bourbon whiskey)
•

PREPARATION
Shake vigorously in a shaker over ice for about
10 seconds and strain into the glass.
Garnish with a maraschino cherry.

Glass: highball glass

1915

*"Long Bar," Raffles Hotel, Singapore. Ngiam Tong Boon
came up with the original sling, which was called the Strait
Sling.*

Tom Collins

↓

2 oz / 6 cl Tanqueray No. TEN Gin
1 oz / 3 cl fresh lemon juice
0.3 oz / 1 cl sugar syrup (see page 222)
3.4 oz / 10 cl soda water
•

GARNISH
¼ Lemon
1 Maraschino cherry
•

PREPARATION
Stir in a highball glass and top up with
soda. Garnish with a lemon wedge and a
maraschino cherry.
•

Glass: highball glass or Collins glass

Twentieth Century

↓

1.4 oz / 4 cl Tanqueray No. TEN Gin
0.7 oz / 2 cl Lillet Blanc
0.7 oz / 2 cl white crème de cacao
0.7 oz / 2 cl fresh lemon juice
•

GARNISH
Lemon zest
•

PREPARATION
Shake vigorously in a shaker over ice for
about 10 seconds and strain into the glass.
Garnish with a lemon twist.

Glass: cocktail coupe

1937

William J. Tarling, Café Royal Cocktail Book

Vesper Martini

↓

1.4 oz / 4 cl Tanqueray No. TEN Gin
0.7 oz / 2 cl Belvedere Vodka
0.3 oz / 1 cl Lillet Blanc
optional: 2 dashes The Bitter Truth
Orange Bitters
•

GARNISH
Lemon zest

PREPARATION

Shake well in a shaker over ice for about 10 seconds, then strain into a glass. Squeeze lemon zest over the drink and drop it into the glass.

•

Glass: highball glass

White Lady

2 oz / 6 cl Tanqueray No. TEN Gin
1 oz / 3 cl fresh lemon juice
0.3 oz / 1 cl sugar syrup (see page 222)
0.7 oz / 2 cl triple sec
1 egg white

•

GARNISH

Lemon zest

•

PREPARATION

Shake well in a shaker over ice for about 10 seconds, then strain into a glass. Squeeze lemon zest over the drink and drop it into the glass.

•

Glass: cocktail coupe

Harry MacElhone, Harry's ABC of Mixing Cocktails

Vodka Cocktails

Vodka isn't dead and never was. It'll stay on the list of the world's most popular spirits, and the famous saying "Vodka pays the bills"—you can make the most money with vodka—fits the bar scene perfectly. Two countries claim this spirit for themselves—Poland or Russia, who do you think invented it first? That question can't really be answered, but in my opinion, both countries make the best vodkas. But a well-known French producer also makes my top 3 list.

As you probably know, vodka is distilled from grain, potatoes or molasses—and lately, grapes are being used too. Rye, wheat and barley are the most popular types in the grain segment. Potato-based vodkas are heavier and sweeter, molasses-based ones are usually cheaper and rarely used in good bars. Cold or hot snacks like pickled mushrooms, pickles, meatballs, mashed potatoes, rye bread and butter, or tart fruit go great with vodka and can be enjoyed while you're sipping.

Black Russian

2 oz / 6 cl Belvedere Vodka
1 oz / 3 cl Kahlúa

•

GARNISH

None

•

PREPARATION

Stir well in a tumbler over ice.

•

Glass: tumbler—Old Fashioned glass

Bloody Mary

2 oz / 6 cl Belvedere Vodka
0.3 oz / 1 cl fresh lemon juice
4 oz / 12 cl top-quality tomato juice
6 dashes Worcestershire sauce
2 dashes Tabasco
1 pinch salt
1 pinch black pepper

•

GARNISH

¼ Lemon

•

PREPARATION

Shake lightly in a shaker for 2 seconds and strain straight into a highball glass without ice. Place a lemon wedge on the drink.

Glass: highball glass

1921

Fernand Petoit, "Harry's New York Bar," Paris

Bullfrog

(This is a slightly tweaked version of the original recipe by me.)

2 oz / 6 cl Belvedere Vodka

4 oz / 12 cl lemonade (preferably homemade lemon lemonade, or Sprite as an alternative)

¼ lime

•

GARNISH

¼ Lime

•

PREPARATION

Stir well in a highball glass. Squeeze a lime wedge over the drink and drop it in the glass.

•

Glass: highball glass

Bullshot

2 oz / 6 cl Belvedere Vodka

0.2 oz / 0.5 cl fresh lemon juice

4 oz / 12 cl beef consommé

6 dashes Worcestershire sauce

2 dashes Tabasco

1 pinch salt

1 pinch black pepper

GARNISH

None

•

PREPARATION

Shake lightly in a shaker for 2 seconds and strain straight into the highball glass without ice.

•

Glass: highball glass

1950s Years

USA

Caipiroska

1 lime

2 bs white cane sugar

2 oz / 6 cl Belvedere Vodka

•

GARNISH

None

•

PREPARATION

Cut the lime into eighths, put it in the glass, sprinkle with sugar and gently muddle. Add crushed ice and vodka. Then stir gently.

•

Glass: tumbler—Old Fashioned glass

Very well known in South America, especially in Brazil.

Cosmopolitan

1.7 oz / 5 cl Belvedere Vodka

0.7 oz / 2 cl fresh lime juice

0.7 oz / 2 cl Cointreau

1.4 oz / 4 cl cranberry juice

•

GARNISH

None

•

PREPARATION

Shake well in a shaker over ice for about 10 seconds, then strain into a glass.

•

Glass: cocktail coupe

1934

The original version from Tony Abou-Ganim, Travelling Mixologists, uses gin instead of vodka and raspberry syrup. The drink made its comeback in the late 1990s thanks to the show Sex and the City.

Godmother

2 oz / 6 cl Belvedere Vodka

1 oz / 3 cl Amaretto

•

GARNISH

None

•

PREPARATION

Stir well in a tumbler over ice.

•

Glass: tumbler—Old Fashioned glass

God's Child

1.7 oz / 5 cl Belvedere Vodka
0.7 oz / 2 cl amaretto
1 oz / 3 cl cream
0.3 oz / 1 cl sugar syrup (see page 222)

•

GARNISH
None

•

PREPARATION
Shake vigorously in a shaker over ice for about 10 seconds and strain into a glass over crushed ice.

•

Glass: cocktail coupe

Greyhound

2 oz / 6 cl Belvedere Vodka
5.4–6.8 oz / 16–20 cl grapefruit juice or grapefruit lemonade

•

GARNISH
⅛ Grapefruit

•

PREPARATION
Stir gently in a highball glass. Place a wedge of grapefruit on the finished drink.

•

Glass: highball glass

Harvey Wallbanger

2 oz / 6 cl Belvedere Vodka
4 oz / 12 cl fresh orange juice
0.3 oz / 1 cl Galliano

•

GARNISH
⅛ Orange

•

PREPARATION
Gently stir vodka and orange juice in the glass. Then float Galliano on top. Place an orange wedge on the finished drink.

•

Glass: highball glass

Moscow Mule

2 oz / 6 cl Belvedere Vodka
5.4–6.8 oz / 16–20 cl ginger beer (see page 148)

•

GARNISH
2 thin slices of cucumber

•

PREPARATION
Stir gently in the glass. Garnish with cucumber slices.

•

Glass: highball glass or copper mug

Smirnoff Distillery

Polar Bear

1.7 oz / 5 cl Belvedere Vodka
1.4 oz / 4 cl cream
0.7 oz / 2 cl white crème de cacao
1 bs lightly whipped cream

•

GARNISH
None

•

PREPARATION
Shake vigorously in a shaker over ice for about 10 seconds and strain into the glass.

•

Glass: cocktail coupe

Salty Dog

2 oz / 6 cl Belvedere Vodka
5.4–6.8 oz / 16–20 cl grapefruit juice or grapefruit lemonade

•

GARNISH
Salt
⅛ Grapefruit

•

PREPARATION
Rim the glass with salt. Gently stir the ingredients in the glass. Place a wedge of grapefruit on the finished drink.

•

Glass: highball glass

Screwdriver

2 oz / 6 cl Belvedere Vodka
5 oz / 15 cl fresh orange juice

•

GARNISH
⅛ Orange

•

PREPARATION
Stir gently in the glass. Place an orange wedge on the finished drink.

•

Glass: highball glass

When American oil workers stationed in the Persian Gulf had no spoons to hand to stir their drinks, they used screwdrivers instead.

Velvet Hammer

1 oz / 3 cl Belvedere Vodka
1 oz / 3 cl brown crème de cacao
1 oz / 3 cl cream
0.3 oz / 1 cl Cointreau

•

GARNISH
None

•

PREPARATION
Shake well in a shaker over ice for about 10 seconds, then strain into a glass.

•

Glass: cocktail coupe

Vodkatini

2.7 oz / 8 cl Belvedere Vodka
2 dashes Noilly Prat Vermouth

•

GARNISH
1 Green olive with pit or
1 Lemon twist

•

PREPARATION
Stir gently in a mixing glass over ice for about 10 seconds, strain into the glass, and garnish with an olive or lemon twist.

•

Glass: martini glass

White Cloud

1.7 oz / 5 cl Belvedere Vodka
1.7 oz / 5 cl top-quality pineapple juice
0.7 oz / 2 cl cream
0.7 oz / 2 cl white crème de cacao

•

GARNISH
None

•

PREPARATION
Shake vigorously in a shaker over ice for about 10 seconds and strain into a glass over crushed ice.

•

Glass: tumbler—Old Fashioned glass

White Russian

1.4 oz / 4 cl Belvedere Vodka
0.7 oz / 2 cl Kahlúa
cream

•

GARNISH
None

•

PREPARATION
Gently stir vodka and Kahlua in the glass and top with lightly whipped cream.

•

Glass: sherry glass

Harper's Magazine

Whisky Cocktails

Whisky, whether it's bourbon or rye, Scotch single malt or blended, Irish whisky, or maybe even a German whiskey—with a good nose and the right products, whisky can be a solid investment. Aged bottlings and products from now-closed distilleries claim particularly high prices. For mixing, we often prefer an American rye whiskey, which has plenty of character and is just perfect for cocktails. The same goes for bourbon, which is slightly sweeter and, unlike rye whiskey, is made with 51 percent corn. Single malts are too precious for me to use in cocktails—they're really meant for sipping neat, but every now and then I like to use a peaty whisky as a float on a whisky cocktail. It takes years of experience to use a single malt in a mixed drink.

Blood and Sand

1.4 oz / 4 cl Scotch whisky
1 oz / 3 cl fresh orange juice
0.7 oz / 2 cl Cherry Heering
0.7 oz / 2 cl red vermouth
1 pinch black pepper

•

GARNISH
None

•

PREPARATION
Shake vigorously in a shaker over ice for about 10 seconds and strain into the glass.

•

Glass: cocktail coupe

1930

Harry Craddock, The Savoy Cocktail Book

Boston Sour

2 oz / 6 cl Bulleit Rye Whiskey
1 oz / 3 cl fresh lemon juice
0.7 oz / 2 cl sugar syrup (see page 222)
1 egg white

•

GARNISH
Maraschino cherry

PREPARATION
Shake vigorously in a shaker over ice for about 10 seconds and strain into the glass. Garnish with a maraschino cherry.

•

Glass: tumbler—Old Fashioned glass

Boulevardier

1 oz / 3 cl Bulleit Bourbon Whiskey
1 oz / 3 cl Campari
1 oz / 3 cl red vermouth

•

GARNISH
Orange zest

•

PREPARATION
Stir gently in the tumbler.
Garnish with orange zest.

•

Glass: tumbler—Old Fashioned glass

1927

Harry MacElhone, Barflies and Cocktails

Bourbon Highball

2 oz / 6 cl Bulleit Bourbon Whiskey
5 oz / 15 cl ginger ale

GARNISH

Long lemon twist

•

PREPARATION

Stir in a highball glass and garnish with lemon zest.

•

Glass: highball glass

———

Brooklyn

2 oz / 6 cl Bulleit Rye Whiskey

0.7 oz / 2 cl dry vermouth

0.5 oz / 1.5 cl Amer Picon

0.3 oz / 1 cl Maraschino

•

GARNISH

Lemon zest

•

PREPARATION

Stir gently in a mixing glass over ice for about 10 seconds, then strain into a glass. Garnish with a lemon twist.

•

Glass: cocktail coupe

1910

Jack Grohusko, Jack's Manual

———

Georgia Mint Julep

2 oz / 6 cl Bulleit Bourbon Whiskey

0.3 oz / 1 cl sugar syrup (see page 222)

0.3 oz / 1 cl apricot brandy

10 mint leaves

•

GARNISH

Mint sprig

•

PREPARATION

Pour sugar syrup over mint leaves in the cup and muddle them. Add whiskey and apricot brandy, fill up with crushed ice and stir. Garnish with a mint sprig.

•

Glass: julep cup

1840

Captain Frederick Marryat, Second Series of a Diary in America

———

Godfather

2 oz / 6 cl Bulleit Bourbon Whiskey

1 oz / 3 cl Amaretto

•

GARNISH

None

•

PREPARATION

Stir well in a tumbler over ice.

•

Glass: tumbler—Old Fashioned glass

———

Golden Nail

2 oz / 6 cl Bulleit Bourbon Whiskey

---

1 oz / 3 cl Southern Comfort

2 dashes The Bitter Truth Orange Bitters

•

GARNISH

None

•

PREPARATION

Stir well in a tumbler over ice.

•

Glass: tumbler—Old Fashioned glass

———

Horse's Neck

2 oz / 6 cl Bulleit Bourbon Whiskey

5 oz / 15 cl ginger ale

5 dashes The Bitter Truth Aromatic Bitters

•

GARNISH

Long lemon twist

•

PREPARATION

Stir in a highball glass and garnish with lemon zest.

•

Glass: highball glass

———

Irish Coffee

1.4 oz / 4 cl Irish whiskey

2 bs brown sugar

1 double espresso

•

GARNISH

Lightly whipped cream

PREPARATION

Heat Irish whiskey with brown sugar until the sugar dissolves. Top up with espresso and garnish with cream.

•

Glass: irish Coffee glass

Joe Sheridan, "Restaurant Foynes"

Little Italy

↓

2 oz / 6 cl Irish Whiskey
0.7 oz / 2 cl red vermouth
0.3 oz / 1 cl Cynar

•

GARNISH

Orange zest

•

PREPARATION

Stir gently in a mixing glass over ice for about 10 seconds, then strain into a glass. Garnish with orange zest.

•

Glass: cocktail coupe

"Pegu Club," New York

London Sour

↓

2 oz / 6 cl Johnnie Walker Gold Label
1 oz / 3 cl fresh lemon juice
0.7 oz / 2 cl sugar syrup (see page 222)

GARNISH

Maraschino cherry

•

PREPARATION

Shake well in a shaker over ice for about 10 seconds, then strain into a glass. Garnish with a maraschino cherry.

•

Glass: tumbler—Old Fashioned glass

Manhattan

↓

2 oz / 6 cl Bulleit Rye Whiskey
1 oz / 3 cl red vermouth
2 dashes The Bitter Truth Orange Bitters

•

GARNISH

Lemon zest

•

PREPARATION

Stir gently in a mixing glass over ice for about 10 seconds, strain into a glass and garnish with lemon zest.

•

Glass: cocktail coupe

Where the drink was invented is still a mystery.

Manhattan Perfect

↓

1.7 oz / 5 cl Bulleit Bourbon Whiskey

0.7 oz / 2 cl red vermouth
0.7 oz / 2 cl dry vermouth
2 dashes The Bitter Truth Aromatic Bitters

•

GARNISH

Maraschino cherry

•

PREPARATION

Stir gently in a mixing glass over ice for about 10 seconds, then strain into a glass. Garnish with a maraschino cherry.

•

Glass: cocktail coupe

Where the drink was invented is still unclear.

Millionaire

↓

1.7 oz / 5 cl Bulleit Bourbon Whiskey
0.7 oz / 2 cl fresh lemon juice
0.3 oz / 1 cl triple sec
0.3 oz / 1 cl grenadine
1 egg white

•

GARNISH

None

•

PREPARATION

Shake vigorously in a shaker over ice for about 10 seconds and strain into the glass.

•

Glass: cocktail coupe

The drink was invented during Prohibition.

Mint Julep

10 mint leaves
0.3 oz / 1 cl sugar syrup (see page 222)
2 oz / 6 cl Bulleit Bourbon Whiskey

•

GARNISH
Mint sprig

•

PREPARATION
Pour sugar syrup over mint leaves in the cup and muddle them. Add whiskey, top up with crushed ice, and stir. Garnish with a mint sprig.

•

Glass: julep cup

1840

Captain Frederick Marryat, Second Series of a Diary in America

---

Morning Glory Fizz

2 oz / 6 cl Johnnie Walker Gold Label
1 oz / 3 cl fresh lemon juice
0.7 oz / 2 cl sugar syrup (see page 222)
1 dash Pernod or absinthe
1 egg white
2–2.7 oz / 6–8 cl soda water

•

GARNISH
¼ Lemon
Maraschino cherry

PREPARATION
Shake in a shaker over ice for about 10 seconds, top up with soda, and strain into the glass. Garnish with a lemon wedge and a maraschino cherry.

•

Glass: highball glass

1900

Harry Johnson, Bartenders' Manual

Mother in Law

2 oz / 6 cl Bulleit Bourbon Whiskey
0.2 oz / 0.5 cl Cointreau
0.2 oz / 0.5 cl Maraschino
0.2 oz / 0.5 cl sugar syrup (see page 222)
0.2 oz / 0.5 cl Amer Picon
2 dashes Peychaud's Bitters or
The Bitter Truth Creole Bitters
2 dashes The Bitter Truth Aromatic Bitters

•

GARNISH
Maraschino cherry

•

PREPARATION
Stir gently in a mixing glass over ice for about 10 seconds, then strain into a glass. Garnish with a maraschino cherry.

•

Glass: martini glass

1895

New Orleans

Nat King Cole

2 oz / 6 cl Bulleit Rye Whiskey
1 oz / 3 cl red vermouth
0.3 oz / 1 cl Fernet Branca
2 dashes The Bitter Truth Orange Bitters
2 oz / 6 cl soda water

•

GARNISH
Orange zest

•

PREPARATION
Stir gently in the tumbler and top up with soda. Garnish with orange zest.

•

Glass: tumbler—Old Fashioned glass

New Yorker

2 oz / 6 cl Bulleit Bourbon Whiskey
½ lime
0.3 oz / 1 cl grenadine

•

GARNISH
Orange zest

•

PREPARATION
Pour bourbon whiskey into the tumbler. Squeeze the lime, float with grenadine, and stir gently. Garnish with orange zest.

•

Glass: tumbler—Old Fashioned glass

Old Fashioned Cocktail

↓

2 oz / 6 cl Bulleit Rye Whiskey

1 sugar cube (alternative: 0.3 oz / 1 cl sugar syrup, see page 222)

2–3 dashes Angostura Bitters

•

GARNISH

Lemon or orange peel

•

PREPARATION

Stir gently in a mixing glass over ice for about 10 seconds and strain into a glass. Squeeze lemon peel over the drink and drop it into the glass.

•

Glass: tumbler—Old Fashioned glass

Theodore Proulx, The Bartender's Manual

Penicillin Cocktail

↓

2 oz / 6 cl Johnnie Walker Gold Label

0.8 oz / 2.5 cl fresh lemon juice

0.7 oz / 2 cl honey–ginger syrup (see page 221)

0.3 oz / 1 cl Scotch Islay whisky

•

GARNISH

⅛ Lemon

Candied ginger

PREPARATION

Shake vigorously in the shaker over ice for about 10 seconds, strain into a glass, and float with whiskey. Garnish with a lemon wedge and ginger.

•

Glass: tumbler—Old Fashioned glass

Sam Ross, "Milk & Honey," New York

Presbyterian

↓

2 oz / 6 cl Bulleit Bourbon Whiskey

3.4 oz / 10 cl ginger ale

1.7 oz / 5 cl club soda

2 dashes The Bitter Truth Aromatic Bitters

•

GARNISH

None

•

PREPARATION

Stir gently in a highball glass.

•

Glass: highball glass

Rattlesnake

↓

2 oz / 6 cl Bulleit Bourbon Whiskey

1 oz / 3 cl fresh lemon juice

0.7 oz / 2 cl sugar syrup (see page 222)

1 dash absinthe

1 egg white

GARNISH

None

•

PREPARATION

Shake vigorously in a shaker over ice for about 10 seconds and strain into the glass.

•

Glass: cocktail coupe

Harry Craddock, The Savoy Cocktail Book "American Bar," Savoy Hotel, London

---

Rusty Nail

↓

2 oz / 6 cl Johnnie Walker Gold Label

1 oz / 3 cl Drambuie

•

GARNISH

None

•

PREPARATION

Stir gently in the tumbler.

•

Glass: tumbler—Old Fashioned glass

Rusty and Dusty Nail

Sazerac

↓

2 dashes absinthe

2 oz / 6 cl Bulleit Rye Whiskey

1 sugar cube (alternative: 0.3 oz / 1 cl sugar
syrup, see page 222)

6 dashes Peychaud's Bitters (alternative: The
Bitter Truth Creole Bitters)

•

GARNISH

Lemon zest

•

PREPARATION

Rinse the tumbler with absinthe. Stir
whiskey, sugar and bitters gently in a mixing
glass for about 10 seconds and strain into
a glass without ice. Garnish with a lemon
twist.

•

Glass: tumbler—Old Fashioned glass

William Boothby, The World Drinks and How to Mix Them

Scoff Law

2 oz / 6 cl Bulleit Rye Whiskey
1 oz / 3 cl dry vermouth
0.3 oz / 1 cl fresh lime juice
2 dashes grenadine
2 dashes The Bitter Truth Orange Bitters

•

GARNISH

Optional: Orange zest

•

PREPARATION

Stir gently in a mixing glass over ice for about
10 seconds, strain into a glass and optionally
garnish with orange zest.

•

Glass: cocktail coupe

Harry MacElhone, Barflies and Cocktails

T.N.T.

1.7 oz / 5 cl Bulleit Bourbon Whiskey
0.7 oz / 2 cl Pernod or absinthe

•

GARNISH

None

•

PREPARATION

Stir gently in the tumbler.

•

Glass: tumbler—Old Fashioned glass

Vieux Carré

1 oz / 3 cl Bulleit Rye Whiskey
1 oz / 3 cl Hennessy VS
1 oz / 3 cl red vermouth
0.2 oz / 0.5 cl Bénédictine
2 dashes The Bitter Truth Aromatic Bitters
2 dashes Peychaud's Bitters or
The Bitter Truth Creole Bitters

•

GARNISH

Optional: Orange zest

•

PREPARATION

Stir gently in a mixing glass over ice for about
10 seconds, then strain into a glass.
Optionally garnish with orange zest.

Glass: tumbler—Old Fashioned glass

Stanley Clisby Arthur, Famous New Orleans Drinks

Waldorf Astoria Eggnog

1.7 oz / 5 cl Bulleit Bourbon Whiskey
0.7 oz / 2 cl tawny port
0.3 oz / 1 cl sugar syrup (see page 222)
2.7 oz / 8 cl milk
0.3 oz / 1 cl cream
2 egg yolks

•

GARNISH

Nutmeg

•

PREPARATION

Shake well in a shaker over ice for about
10 seconds, then strain into a glass. Grate
nutmeg over the finished drink.

•

Glass: Highball glass or eggnog glass

Albert Stevens Crockett, The Old Waldorf-Astoria Barbook

Whiskey Smash

2 oz / 6 cl Bulleit Rye Whiskey
1 oz / 3 cl fresh lemon juice

0.7 oz / 2 cl sugar syrup (see page 222)

10 mint leaves

•

GARNISH

Mint sprig

•

PREPARATION

Shake vigorously in a shaker over ice for about 10 seconds and strain into a glass over crushed ice. Garnish with a sprig of mint.

•

Glass: tumbler—Old Fashioned glass

Harry Johnson

Whiskey Sour

2 oz / 6 cl Bulleit Rye Whiskey

1 oz / 3 cl fresh lemon juice

0.7 oz / 2 cl sugar syrup (see page 222)

•

GARNISH

Maraschino cherry

•

PREPARATION

Shake vigorously in a shaker over ice for about 10 seconds and strain into a glass. Garnish with a maraschino cherry.

•

Glass: tumbler—Old Fashioned glass

Wisconsin newspaper

Tequila cocktails

Gone are the days when when that bottle with the little Mexican hat from the supermarket was our only chance to experience the taste and buzz of tequila. "100 percent agave" are the magic words on the label, already pointing out that the spirit is made from the heart of the blue agave with no artificial additives at all. It's obvious in the taste, too, once you try one of these spirits. Neat or in cocktails, both are a treat. Salt, cinnamon, lemons and limes, biting or licking, all have fallen out of favor because they would simply drown out the awesome flavors of a good tequila. Blanco, Reposado, Anejo, and Extra-Anejo are the four aging levels of tequila. We usually use Blanco and Reposado for mixing, and drink Anejo and Extra-Anejo mostly neat. The legendary caterpillar—not a worm, as people always claim—is found not in tequila bottles, but in mezcal. Tequila, 80 percent of which comes from the state of Jalisco, is one of the biggest spirits on the market, with over 900 types and more than 130 producers.

Brave Bull

1.4 oz / 4 cl Don Julio Blanco Tequila

0.7 oz / 2 cl Tia Maria

•

TOPPING

1 tbsp lightly whipped cream

•

GARNISH

None

•

PREPARATION

Stir tequila and Tia Maria gently in a mixing glass over ice for about 10 seconds and strain into a glass. Then float the lightly whipped cream on top.

•

Glass: sherry glass

Chapala

1.7 oz / 5 cl Don Julio Blanco Tequila

0.7 oz / 2 cl fresh lemon juice

0.2 oz / 0.5 cl grenadine

0.2 oz / 0.5 cl triple sec

2 oz / 6 cl orange juice

GARNISH

⅛ Orange

•

PREPARATION

Shake in a shaker over ice for about 10 seconds, then strain into a highball glass over crushed ice. Garnish with an orange wedge.

•

Glass: highball glass

El Diablo

1.7 oz / 5 cl Don Julio Blanco Tequila

0.3 oz / 1 cl fresh lime juice

5 oz / 15 cl ginger beer (see page 148) or ginger ale

0.3 oz / 1 cl crème de cassis

•

GARNISH

¼ Lime

•

PREPARATION

Carefully stir tequila, lime juice, and ginger beer in a highball glass. Then float crème de cassis on top and add the lime wedge.

•

Glass: highball glass

1946

Victor Bergeron, Trader Vic's Book of Food and Drink

Estilo Viejo

2 oz / 6 cl Don Julio Reposado Tequila

0.3 oz / 1 cl agave syrup

2 dashes The Bitter Truth Aromatic Bitters

•

GARNISH

Grapefruit zest

•

PREPARATION

Stir gently in a mixing glass over ice for about 10 seconds, then strain into a glass. Garnish with grapefruit zest.

•

Glass: tumbler—Old Fashioned glass

2005

Henry Besant & Andres Masso, Margarita Rocks

Margarita

2 oz / 6 cl Don Julio Blanco Tequila

0.7 oz / 2 cl fresh lime juice

0.7 oz / 2 cl triple sec

•

GARNISH

Salt

•

PREPARATION

Rim the glass with salt. Shake all ingredients in a shaker over ice for about 10 seconds, then strain into a glass.

•

Glass: cocktail coupe

1953

Esquire Magazine

Mexicana

2 oz / 6 cl Don Julio Blanco Tequila

1.4 oz / 4 cl top-quality pineapple juice

0.7 oz / 2 cl fresh lemon juice

0.3 oz / 1 cl grenadine

•

GARNISH

None

•

PREPARATION

Shake vigorously in a shaker over ice for about 10 seconds and strain into the glass.

•

Glass: tumbler—Old Fashioned glass

1987

Mike Colani, "Steppenwolf," Hamburg

Paloma

1.7 oz / 5 cl Don Julio Blanco Tequila

5 oz / 15 cl grapefruit lemonade

0.7 oz / 2 cl fresh lime juice

1 bs fleur de sel

•

GARNISH

Grapefruit zest

PREPARATION

Carefully stir in a highball glass and garnish with grapefruit zest.

•

Glass: highball glass

1953

Esquire Magazine

Picador

↓

2 oz / 6 cl Don Julio Blanco Tequila
0.7 oz / 2 cl fresh lime or lemon juice
0.7 oz / 2 cl Cointreau

•

GARNISH

None

•

PREPARATION

Shake vigorously in a shaker over ice for about 10 seconds and strain into the glass.

•

Glass: cocktail coupe

1937

William J. Tarling, Café Royal Cocktail Book

Rosita

↓

1.4 oz / 4 cl Don Julio Blanco Tequila
0.3 oz / 1 cl Campari
0.3 oz / 1 cl dry vermouth

0.3 oz / 1 cl red vermouth
2 dashes The Bitter Truth Aromatic Bitters

•

TOPPING

Soda water

•

GARNISH

None

•

PREPARATION

Stir gently in a mixing glass over ice for about 10 seconds, strain into a glass, and top with soda.

•

Glass: cocktail coupe

1988

Leo Cotton, Old Mr. Boston De Luxe Official Bartender's Guide

---

South of the Border

↓

1.4 oz / 4 cl Don Julio Blanco Tequila
0.7 oz / 2 cl Tia Maria
0.7 oz / 2 cl fresh lime juice

•

GARNISH

None

•

PREPARATION

Stir gently in the tumbler.

•

Glass: tumbler—Old Fashioned glass

Tequila Matador

↓

1.4 oz / 4 cl Don Julio Blanco Tequila
0.3 oz / 1 cl triple sec
0.7 oz / 2 cl fresh lime juice
0.3 oz / 1 cl sugar syrup (see page 222)
0.7 oz / 2 cl top-quality pineapple juice

•

GARNISH

Pineapple slice

•

PREPARATION

Shake vigorously in a shaker over ice for about 10 seconds and strain into a glass over crushed ice. Garnish with pineapple.

•

Glass: tumbler—Old Fashioned glass

Tequila Mockingbird

↓

1.7 oz / 5 cl Don Julio Blanco Tequila
0.3 oz / 1 cl crème de menthe verte
0.7 oz / 2 cl fresh lime juice
1.7 oz / 5 cl soda water

•

GARNISH

None

•

PREPARATION

Stir gently in the tumbler.

•

Glass: tumbler—Old Fashioned glass

Tommy's Margarita

2 oz / 6 cl Don Julio Blanco Tequila
1 oz / 3 cl fresh lime juice
0.7 oz / 2 cl agave nectar or syrup

•

GARNISH
None

•

PREPARATION
Shake vigorously in a shaker over ice for about 10 seconds and strain into the glass.

•

Glass: tumbler—Old Fashioned glass

"Tommy's Restaurant," San Francisco

Toreador

2 oz / 6 cl Don Julio Blanco Tequila
1 oz / 3 cl apricot brandy
1 oz / 3 cl fresh lime juice

•

GARNISH
Salt

•

PREPARATION
Rim the glass with salt. Carefully stir the ingredients in a tumbler. Shake vigorously in a shaker over ice for about 10 seconds and strain into the glass.

•

Glass: cocktail coupe

1937

William J. Tarling, Café Royal Cocktail Book

Rum Cocktails

The first rum cocktail that comes to most people's minds is the classic Mojito. That's totally justified, because this creation is the most popular rum cocktail worldwide and is also one of my favorite drinks—as long as it's made right. Rum is distilled from molasses, except for rhum agricole, which is made from fresh sugarcane juice—and when it's used for a Ti Punch Cocktail, it's totally worth sinning for. Invented in the Caribbean in the 17th century, rum has all sorts of spellings; it's also known as ron or rhum, and was first mentioned by the Jamaican governor as "rum-bullion." Royal Navy sailors, who still received a daily "rum ration" until 1970, drank their rum with hot water. This classic seafarer's drink made its way into cocktail history as "grog." 1940 onwards marked the era of classic tiki cocktails. They are based on dark rum, which has a slightly sweeter note and, when made and aged properly, is an absolute treat even solo.

Algonquin

2 oz / 6 cl white rum
0.7 oz / 2 cl fresh lime juice
0.3 oz / 1 cl Bénédictine
0.3 oz / 1 cl Chambord

•

GARNISH
None

•

PREPARATION
Shake well in a shaker over ice for about 10 seconds, then strain into a glass.

•

Glass: cocktail coupe

Apricot Lady

2 oz / 6 cl white rum
0.7 oz / 2 cl fresh lemon juice
0.7 oz / 2 cl apricot brandy
1 egg white

•

GARNISH
None

•

PREPARATION
Shake well in a shaker over ice for about 10 seconds, then strain into a glass.

•

Bacardi Cocktail

2 oz / 6 cl Bacardi White
0.7 oz / 2 cl fresh lime juice
0.3 oz / 1 cl grenadine

•

GARNISH
None

•

PREPARATION
Shake well in a shaker over ice for about 10
seconds, then strain into a glass.

•

Glass: cocktail coupe

1917

Tom Bullock, The Ideal Bartender

Baltimore Eggnog

FOR 10 PEOPLE
10 eggs
2.7 oz / 8 cl sugar syrup (see page 222)
1 small bs grated nutmeg
8.4 oz / 25 cl jamaican rum
3.4 oz / 10 cl madeira
101 oz / 3 l whole milk (3.5%)

•

GARNISH
Nutmeg

PREPARATION
Beat the egg yolks with sugar syrup and
nutmeg until frothy. Beat the egg whites
until stiff and fold them in, gradually add the
alcohol, and finally mix in the milk bit by bit.
Grate nutmeg over the finished drink.

•

Glass: champagne glass

1862

Jerry Thomas, How to Mix Drinks

Banana Daiquiri

¼ banana
2 oz / 6 cl white rum
1 oz / 3 cl fresh lime juice
0.3 oz / 1 cl banana syrup
0.3 oz / 1 cl sugar syrup (see page 222)

•

GARNISH
None

•

PREPARATION
Muddle the banana in the shaker. Add the rest
of the ingredients and ice, shake well for about
10 seconds, and strain into the glass.

•

Glass: cocktail coupe

1953

George Soule, St. Thomas, Virgin Islands

Beachcomber

2 oz / 6 cl white rum
1 oz / 3 cl fresh lime juice
0.7 oz / 2 cl triple sec
0.3 oz / 1 cl Maraschino

•

GARNISH
None

•

PREPARATION
Shake well in a shaker over ice for about 10
seconds, then strain into a glass.

•

Glass: cocktail coupe

1937

William J. Tarling, Café Royal Cocktail Book

Bee's Kiss

1.4 oz / 4 cl white rum
0.7 oz / 2 cl dark rum
0.7 oz / 2 cl cream
0.7 oz / 2 cl honey syrup (see page 221)

•

GARNISH
None

•

PREPARATION
Shake vigorously in a shaker over ice for
about 10 seconds and strain into the glass.

•

Glass: cocktail coupe

Between the Sheets

↓

1 oz / 3 cl white rum
1 oz / 3 cl brandy
1 oz / 3 cl Cointreau
0.5 oz / 1.5 cl lemon juice

•

GARNISH
None

•

PREPARATION
Shake vigorously in a shaker over ice for about 10 seconds and strain into the glass.

•

Glass: cocktail coupe

1920s Years

Harry MacElhone, "Harry's New York Bar," Paris

Caipirissima

↓

½ lime
2 bs white cane sugar
6 seedless grapes
2 oz / 6 cl Jamaican rum

•

TOPPING
4 cl soda water

•

GARNISH
None

PREPARATION
Quarter the lime and muddle it with cane sugar and the grapes in the shaker. Add the rum and shake hard over ice for about 10 seconds. Pour into the tumbler and top it off with soda water.

•

Glass: tumbler—Old Fashioned glass

2002

Dale DeGroff, The Craft of the Cocktail

Canchanchara

↓

2 oz / 6 cl dark rum
1 oz / 3 cl fresh lime juice
0.7 oz / 2 cl honey syrup (see page 221)

•

GARNISH
None

•

PREPARATION
Shake vigorously in a shaker over ice for about 10 seconds and strain into the glass.

•

Glass: tumbler—Old Fashioned glass

1862

Jerry Thomas, How to Mix Drinks

Continental

↓

1.7 oz / 5 cl white rum

0.3 oz / 1 cl crème de menthe verte
0.7 oz / 2 cl fresh lime juice
0.3 oz / 1 cl sugar syrup (see page 222)

•

GARNISH
None

•

PREPARATION
Shake vigorously in a shaker over ice for about 10 seconds and strain into the glass.

•

Glass: tumbler—Old Fashioned glass

Creole

↓

1.7 oz / 5 cl white rum
0.3 oz / 1 cl fresh lemon juice
3.4 oz / 10 cl beef consommé
2 dashes Tabasco
6 dashes Worcestershire sauce
salt and pepper

•

GARNISH
None

•

PREPARATION
Stir gently in a highball glass.

•

Glass: highball glass

Cuba Libre

↓

1.7 oz / 5 cl white rum
5 oz / 15 cl Coca-Cola
2 lime wedges

GARNISH

None

•

PREPARATION

Stir gently in a highball glass.

•

Glass: highball glass

1937

Eleanor Early, Ports of the Sun: A Guide to the Caribbean, Bermuda, Nassau, Havana and Panama

Daiquiri

2 oz / 6 cl white rum
1 oz / 3 cl fresh lime juice
0.7 oz / 2 cl sugar syrup (see page 222)

GARNISH

None

•

PREPARATION

Shake vigorously in a shaker over ice for about 10 seconds and strain into the glass.

•

Glass: cocktail coupe

"El Floridita Bar," Havana

Daiquiri el Floridita

2 oz / 6 cl white rum

0.7 oz / 2 cl fresh lime juice
0.3 oz / 1 cl sugar syrup (see page 222)
0.3 oz / 1 cl Maraschino
1 oz / 3 cl pink grapefruit juice

GARNISH

Grapefruit zest

•

PREPARATION

Shake vigorously in a shaker over ice for about 10 seconds and strain into a glass. Garnish with grapefruit zest.

•

Glass: cocktail coupe

"El Floridita Bar," Havana

Dark & Stormy

2 oz / 6 cl Gosling's Black Seal Rum
5 oz / 15 cl ginger beer

GARNISH

none

•

PREPARATION

Stir gently in a highball glass.

•

Glass: highball glass

Official national drink of the Bermuda Islands

El Presidente

2 oz / 6 cl cuban rum

---

1 oz / 3 cl dry vermouth
0.2 oz / 0.5 cl orange curaçao
0.2 oz / 0.5 cl grenadine

•

GARNISH

Orange zest

•

PREPARATION

Stir gently in a mixing glass over ice for about 10 seconds, then strain into a glass. Garnish with orange zest.

•

Glass: martini glass

1920s Years

Havana

Fish House Punch

25.4 oz / 750 ml dark rum
11.8 oz / 350 ml cognac
2 oz / 60 ml peach brandy
11.8 oz / 350 ml fresh lime juice
28.7 oz / 850 ml water
8.5 oz / 250 ml sugar syrup (see page 222)

GARNISH

None

•

PREPARATION

Stir in the tumbler, let it sit for at least 3 hours, and then serve.

•

Glass: tumbler—Old Fashioned glass or heat-resistant beaker

1732

The Colony in Schuylkill, Philadelphia

Fog Cutter

1.4 oz / 4 cl Puerto Rican rum
0.7 oz / 2 cl brandy
0.3 oz / 1 cl gin
0.7 oz / 2 cl almond syrup
0.7 oz / 2 cl freshly squeezed lemon juice
0.7 oz / 2 cl freshly squeezed orange juice
0.7 oz / 2 cl cream sherry

•

GARNISH
None

•

PREPARATION
Shake vigorously in a shaker over ice for about 10 seconds, float with sherry.

•

Glass: highball glass

1946

Victor Bergeron,
Trader Vic's Book of Food and Drink

Gansevoort Fizz

1.4 oz / 4 cl dark rum
0.7 oz / 2 cl Drambuie
0.7 oz / 2 cl fresh lime juice

---

2 dashes Peychaud's Bitters or
The Bitter Truth Creole Bitters

•

TOPPING
3.4 oz / 10 cl soda water

•

GARNISH
Lemon zest

•

PREPARATION
Shake vigorously in a shaker over ice for about 10 seconds, strain into a glass and top with soda water. Garnish with a twist of lemon zest.

•

Glass: highball glass

Grog

1.7 oz / 5 cl dark rum
0.7 oz / 2 cl fresh lime juice
0.7 oz / 2 cl demerara syrup (see page 221)
1.7 oz / 5 cl hot water
2 dashes The Bitter Truth Aromatic Bitters

•

GARNISH
Orange zest, studded with 3 cloves

•

PREPARATION
Stir gently in a grog glass.
Garnish with orange zest.

•

Glass: heat-resistant grog glass

1781

Thomas Trotter, "Written on board the Berwick,"
in: Notes & Queries, Series 1

Habana Libre

2 oz / 6 cl white rum
0.7 oz / 2 cl fresh lime juice
0.3 oz / 1 cl grenadine

•

GARNISH
Lime zest

•

PREPARATION
Pour into a highball glass, fill up with crushed ice, and stir gently. Garnish with lime zest.

•

Glass: highball glass

Havana Special

1.7 oz / 5 cl white rum
0.3 oz / 1 cl Maraschino
2 oz / 6 cl top quality pineapple juice
2 dashes The Bitter Truth Orange Bitters

•

GARNISH
None

•

PREPARATION
Shake vigorously in a shaker over ice for about 10 seconds and strain over crushed ice.

•

Glass: tumbler—Old Fashioned glass

Hot Buttered Rum

2 oz / 6 cl dark rum
0.3 oz / 1 cl honey syrup (see page 221)
4 oz / 12 cl hot water
1 cinnamon stick
4 small flakes of butter (if available: spiced butter)

•

GARNISH

Orange zest

•

PREPARATION

Stir gently in a grog glass, top with butter. Garnish with orange zest.

•

Glass: heat-resistant grog glass

———

Hot Jamaican

1.7 oz / 5 cl dark rum
0.7 oz / 2 cl fresh lime juice
0.3 oz / 1 cl sugar syrup (see page 222)
1 cinnamon stick
2 oz / 6 cl hot water

•

GARNISH

Lime slice, studded with 3 cloves

•

PREPARATION

Stir gently in the grog glass and garnish with a lime slice.

•

Glass: heat-resistant grog glass

Hotel Nacional Special

2 oz / 6 cl dark rum
0.5 oz / 1.5 cl fresh lime juice
0.5 oz / 1.5 cl sugar syrup (see page 222)
1 oz / 3 cl best quality pineappple juice
0.3 oz / 1 cl Apricot Brandy

•

GARNISH

Lime slice

•

PREPARATION

Shake well in a shaker over ice for about 10 seconds, then strain into a glass. Garnish with a lime slice.

•

Glass: cocktail coupe

Ross Bolton, Bar La Florida Cocktails

———

Hurricane

2 oz / 6 cl white rum
2 oz / 6 cl dark rum
1 oz / 3 cl fresh orange juice
1 oz / 3 cl fresh lime juice
2 oz / 6 cl best quality passion fruit juice
0.5 oz / 1.5 cl sugar syrup (see page 222)
0.5 oz / 1.5 cl grenadine

•

GARNISH

Orange slice with maraschino cherry

PREPARATION

Shake well in a shaker over ice for about 10 seconds, then strain into a glass. Garnish with an orange slice and a maraschino cherry.

•

Glass: hurricane glass

Pat O'Brien, "Mr. O'Brien's Club Tipperary," New Orleans

———

La Floridita Cocktail

1.7 oz / 5 cl white rum
0.7 oz / 2 cl red vermouth
0.7 oz / 2 cl fresh lime juice
0.3 oz / 1 cl white crème de cacao
0.3 oz / 1 cl grenadine

•

GARNISH

None

•

PREPARATION

Shake vigorously in a shaker over ice for about 10 seconds and strain into the glass.

•

Glass: cocktail coupe

———

Mai Tai

("Don the Beachcomber")

1.4 oz / 4 cl dark rum
1 oz / 3 cl gold rum

0.7 oz / 2 cl fresh lime juice
1 oz / 3 cl fresh pink grapefruit juice
0.3 oz / 1 cl The Bitter Truth Golden Falernum
0.5 oz / 1.5 cl Cointreau
0.2 oz / 0.5 cl absinthe
2 dashes The Bitter Truth Aromatic Bitters

•

GARNISH
Mint sprig
Lime zest

•

PREPARATION
Shake well in a shaker over ice for about 10 seconds, then strain into a glass. Garnish with a mint sprig and lime zest.

•

Glass: highball glass

1933

"Don the Beachcomber," Huntington Beach

Mai Tai

(Trader Vic's)

2 oz / 6 cl dark rum
0.5 oz / 1.5 cl orange curaçao
1 oz / 3 cl fresh lime juice
0.3 oz / 1 cl almond syrup
0.2 oz / 0.5 cl sugar syrup (see page 222)

•

GARNISH
Mint sprig
¼ Lime

•

PREPARATION
Shake vigorously in a shaker over ice for about 10 seconds and strain into the glass. Garnish with a mint sprig and lime.

Glass: tumbler—Old Fashioned glass

1944

Victor Bergeron, Trader Vic's Book of Food and Drink

Mary Pickford

2 oz / 6 cl white rum
1.4 oz / 4 cl top-quality pineapple juice
0.3 oz / 1 cl Maraschino
0.2 oz / 0.5 cl grenadine

•

GARNISH
None

•

PREPARATION
Shake vigorously in a shaker over ice for about 10 seconds and strain into the glass.

•

Glass: cocktail coupe

1928

Pedro Chicote, Cocktails

Milk Punch

1 oz / 3 cl dark rum
1 oz / 3 cl Hennessy Cognac
0.7 oz / 2 cl sugar syrup (see page 222)
1.5 oz / 4.5 cl whole milk (3.5%)

•

GARNISH
Nutmeg

PREPARATION
Stir gently in a mixing glass over ice for about 10 seconds, then strain into a glass. Grate nutmeg over the finished drink.

•

Glass: tumbler—Old Fashioned glass

1862

Jerry Thomas, The Bar-Tender's Guide

Mojito

1.7 oz / 5 cl white rum
10 mint leaves
1 oz / 3 cl fresh lime juice
3 bs cane sugar or 0.7 oz / 2 cl sugar syrup (see page 222)
2 oz / 6 cl soda water

•

GARNISH
None

•

PREPARATION
Stir gently in a highball glass. Add ice.

•

Glass: highball glass

1833

Ramón de Palma, El Colera en la Habana, known as El Draquecito

Mulata

2 oz / 6 cl dark rum
1 oz / 3 cl fresh lime juice
0.5 oz / 1.5 cl brown crème de cacao
0.3 oz / 1 cl sugar syrup (see page 222)

GARNISH
None

PREPARATION
Shake vigorously in a shaker over ice for about
10 seconds and strain into the glass.

Glass: cocktail coupe

"El Floridita Bar," Havana

Old Cuban

1.7 oz / 5 cl dark rum
1 oz / 3 cl fresh lime juice
0.7 oz / 2 cl sugar syrup (see page 222)
2 dashes The Bitter Truth Aromatic Bitters
6 mint leaves

TOPPING
3.4 oz / 10 cl Moët & Chandon Brut Champagne

GARNISH
Mint sprig

PREPARATION
Shake vigorously in a shaker over ice for
about 10 seconds and top with champagne.
Garnish with a mint sprig.

Glass: cocktail coupe

2002

Audrey Saunders, New York

Piña Colada

1.7 oz / 5 cl Puerto Rican white rum
1.4 oz / 4 cl coconut cream
4 medium pieces pineapple, peeled

GARNISH
Pineapple leaf

PREPARATION
Blend for 10 seconds over crushed ice in an
electric blender and strain into the glass.
Decorate with a pineapple leaf.

Glass: tumbler—Old Fashioned glass

1949

*"Caribe Hilton's Beachcomber Bar,"
Caribe Hilton Hotel, Puerto Rico*

Planter's Punch
Trader Vic's

3 oz / 9 cl dark rum
1 oz / 3 cl fresh lime juice
0.5 oz / 1.5 cl lemon juice
0.5 oz / 1.5 cl grenadine

0.3 oz / 1 cl sugar syrup (see page 222)
2 oz / 6 cl soda water

GARNISH
None

PREPARATION
Shake vigorously in a shaker over ice for about
10 seconds and strain into the glass.

Glass: highball glass

1946

Victor Bergeron, Trader Vic's Book of Food and Drink

Presidente

1.7 oz / 5 cl white rum
0.7 oz / 2 cl red vermouth
0.3 oz / 1 cl dry vermouth
0.2 oz / 0.5 cl grenadine

GARNISH
Maraschino cherry

PREPARATION
Stir gently in a mixing glass over ice for about
10 seconds, then strain into a glass. Garnish
with a maraschino cherry.

Glass: tumbler—Old Fashioned glass

Queen's Park Swizzle

2 oz / 6 cl Trinidad dark rum
1 oz / 3 cl fresh lime juice
0.7 oz / 2 cl sugar syrup (see page 222)
10 mint leaves
4 dashes The Bitter Truth Aromatic Bitters
0.7 oz / 2 cl soda water

•

GARNISH
Mint sprig

•

PREPARATION

In the tumbler, use a "Swizzle Stick" or a bar spoon to swizzle or stir until a layer of ice forms around the glass. Garnish with a mint sprig.

•

Glass: highball glass

"Queen's Park Hotel," Trinidad

Ribalaigua Daiquiri

1.7 oz / 5 cl white rum
0.7 oz / 2 cl fresh pink grapefruit juice
0.3 oz / 1 cl fresh lime juice
0.3 oz / 1 cl Maraschino

•

GARNISH
None

•

PREPARATION

Shake vigorously in a shaker over ice for about 10 seconds and strain into the glass.

•

Glass: cocktail coupe

1940s Years

Constantino Ribalaigua

Royal Bermuda Yacht Club

2 oz / 6 cl Barbados dark rum
1 oz / 3 cl fresh lime juice
0.5 oz / 1.5 cl The Bitter Truth Golden Falernum
0.2 oz / 0.5 cl Cointreau or triple sec
2 dashes The Bitter Truth Aromatic Bitters

•

GARNISH
Lime zest

•

PREPARATION

Stir gently in a mixing glass over ice for about 10 seconds, then strain into a glass. Garnish with lime zest.

•

Glass: cocktail coupe

1947

Victor Bergeron, Trader Vic's Bartender's Guide

Sloppy Joe

1.7 oz / 5 cl white rum
0.7 oz / 2 cl dry vermouth
0.7 oz / 2 cl fresh lime juice
0.3 oz / 1 cl triple sec
0.3 oz / 1 cl grenadine

•

GARNISH
None

•

PREPARATION

Shake vigorously in a shaker over ice for about 10 seconds and strain into the glass.

•

Glass: cocktail coupe

1933

Sloppy Joe, Sloppy Joe's Cocktail Manual

Ti Punch

1 lime
2 oz / 6 cl rhum agricole
2 bs white cane sugar
or 0.7 oz / 2 cl sugar syrup (see page 222)

•

GARNISH
None

•

PREPARATION

Quarter the lime, place all the ingredients in the tumbler, and stir gently.

Glass: tumbler—Old Fashioned glass

From the French-speaking Caribbean islands

Tom & Jerry

FOR 10 PEOPLE

1.4 oz / 4 cl Jamaican dark rum

12 eggs

2 bs ground cinnamon

1 bs ground cloves

1 bs ground allspice

1.8 oz / 50 g sugar

•

PER GLASS ADDITIONALLY

2 oz / 6 cl Jamaican dark rum

hot water

•

GARNISH

Nutmeg

•

PREPARATION

Mix the ingredients above into a batter. For each serving, pour rum and a portion of the egg mixture into the glass and top up with hot water. Grate nutmeg on top and serve right away.

•

Glass: heat-resistant grog glass

1862

Jerry Thomas, , How to Mix Drinks

West Indies Punch

1 oz / 3 cl dark rum

1 oz / 3 cl white rum

0.7 oz / 2 cl Hennessy Cognac

1 oz / 3 cl madeira

1 oz / 3 cl fresh lime juice

1.7 oz / 5 cl green tea

1.4 oz / 4 cl hot water

0.3 oz / 1 cl sugar syrup (see page 222)

2 bs guava jam

2 dashes The Bitter Truth Aromatic Bitters

•

GARNISH

Nutmeg

•

PREPARATION

Shake well in a shaker over ice for about 10 seconds, then strain into a glass. Grate nutmeg over the finished drink.

•

Glass: highball glass

1946

Victor Bergeron, Trader Vic's Book of Food and Drink

Zombie

1 oz / 3 cl dark rum

1 oz / 3 cl Jamaican dark rum

1 oz / 3 cl Puerto Rican gold rum

0.3 oz / 1 cl The Bitter Truth Golden Falernum

0.7 oz / 2 cl Maraschino

0.7 oz / 2 cl fresh lime juice

0.7 oz / 2 cl fresh pink grapefruit juice

1.5 oz / 4.5 cl pineapple juice of best quality

0.2 oz / 0.5 cl absinthe

0.2 oz / 0.5 cl grenadine

2 dashes The Bitter Truth Aromatic Bitters

•

GARNISH

Mint sprig

•

PREPARATION

Blend with crushed ice in an electric mixer for 10 seconds and strain into the glass. Garnish with a mint sprig.

•

Glass: highball glass

1934

"Don the Beachcomber," Huntington Beach

Cognac & Brandy Cocktails

ognac is one of my most favorite spirits, excellent not only for sipping, but also for mixing in cocktails. It has rather a fusty reputation as an old man's drink served in large snifters, but in fact that's not fair at all, because no spirit is more complex and full of nuance than cognac. Made exclusively from Ugni Blanc white grapes and produced in the Grande Champagne region, cognac is a supreme treat. The grape varieties Folle Blanche and Colombard are quite rare, making up only about ten percent of the production. The other growing regions, including Petite Champagne, Borderies, Fins Bois, Bons Bois, and Bois Ordinaires, also produce magnificent brandies, but these are usually designed for blending from the outset. Although German Weinbrand is also known as brandy, here we're mainly talking about Spanish brandy. After all, Spain has the longest tradition of brandy distilling in Europe, and is also the biggest brandy producer in the world. The three aging levels of Solera, Solera Reserva, and Solera Gran Reserva also reflect brandy's three quality levels. Generally aged in American oak barrels previously used for sherry, brandy adds wonderful flavor to cocktails, too.

B & B

1.4 oz / 4 cl brandy
0.7 oz / 2 cl Bénédictine
0.7 oz / 2 cl sugar syrup (see page 222)
1.5 oz / 4.5 cl whole milk (3.5%)

•

GARNISH

Lemon zest

•

PREPARATION

Stir gently in a tumbler.
Garnish with a lemon twist.

•

Glass: tumbler—Old Fashioned glass

1937

"Club 21," New York

Brandy Alexander

1.7 oz / 5 cl Hennessy Cognac or brandy
0.8 oz / 2.5 cl brown crème de cacao
0.8 oz / 2.5 cl cream

•

GARNISH

Nutmeg

PREPARATION

Shake in a shaker over ice for about 10 seconds. Shake well and strain into the glass. Grate nutmeg over the finished drink.

•

Glass: cocktail coupe

1927

Harry MacElhone, Barflies and Cocktails

Brandy Crusta

2 oz / 6 cl Hennessy Cognac or brandy
0.3 oz / 1 cl fresh lemon juice
0.2 oz / 0.5 cl sugar syrup (see page 222)
0.2 oz / 0.5 cl orange curaçao
2 dashes The Bitter Truth Aromatic Bitters

•

GARNISH

Sugar
Lemon zest

•

PREPARATION

Rim the glass with sugar. Shake the ingredients in a shaker over ice for about 10 seconds and strain into the glass. Garnish with a lemon twist.

•

Glass: sour glass or cocktail coupe

1862

Jerry Thomas, The Bar-Tender's Guide

Brandy Punch

↓

2.4 oz / 7 cl Hennessy Cognac or brandy
1 oz / 3 cl fresh lemon juice
0.3 oz / 1 cl sugar syrup (see page 222)
0.3 oz / 1 cl raspberry syrup
1 handful seasonal berries

GARNISH
None

•

PREPARATION
Shake vigorously in a shaker over ice for about
10 seconds and strain into the glass.

•

Glass: tumbler—Old Fashioned glass

1887

Jerry Thomas, The Bar-Tender's Guide

Coffee Cocktail

↓

1 oz / 3 cl Hennessy Cognac or brandy
1.4 oz / 4 cl port wine
0.2 oz / 0.5 cl sugar syrup (see page 222)
1 egg

•

GARNISH
Nutmeg

PREPARATION
Shake well in a shaker over ice for about
10 seconds, then strain into a glass. Grate
nutmeg over the finished drink.

•

Glass: cocktail coupe

1887

Jerry Thomas, The Bar-Tender's Guide

Corpse Reviver No. 1

↓

1 oz / 3 cl Hennessy Cognac or brandy
1 oz / 3 cl calvados
1 oz / 3 cl red vermouth

•

GARNISH
None

•

PREPARATION
Stir gently in a mixing glass over ice for about
10 seconds, then strain into a glass.

•

Glass: cocktail coupe

1936

Frank Meier, The Artistry of Mixing Drinks

Corpse Reviver No. 3

↓

1 oz / 3 cl Hennessy Cognac or brandy
1 oz / 3 cl Fernet Branca
1 oz / 3 cl Crème de Menthe Blanche

•

GARNISH
None

•

PREPARATION
Stir gently in a mixing glass over ice for about
10 seconds, then strain into a glass.

•

Glass: cocktail coupe

Delmonico

↓

0.7 oz / 2 cl Hennessy Cognac
1 oz / 3 cl Tanqueray No. TEN Gin
0.5 oz / 1.5 cl red vermouth
0.5 oz / 1.5 cl dry vermouth
2 dashes The Bitter Truth Aromatic Bitters

•

GARNISH
Lemon zest

•

PREPARATION
Stir gently in a mixing glass over ice for about
10 seconds, then strain into a glass.
Garnish with a lemon twist.

•

Glass: cocktail coupe

"Delmonico's Restaurant," New York

East India Cocktail

↓

2.4 oz / 7 cl Hennessy Cognac
0.2 oz / 0.5 cl pineapple syrup
0.2 oz / 0.5 cl orange curaçao
0.1 oz / 0.25 cl Maraschino
4 dashes The Bitter Truth Aromatic Bitters

•

GARNISH

Lemon zest

•

PREPARATION

Stir gently in a mixing glass over ice for about 10 seconds, then strain into a glass. Garnish with a lemon twist.

•

Glass: martini glass

1882

Harry Johnson, Bartenders' Manual

———

Fedora Punch

↓

1 oz / 3 cl Hennessy Cognac
0.7 oz / 2 cl Bulleit Bourbon Whiskey
1 oz / 3 cl dark rum
0.7 oz / 2 cl orange curaçao
1 oz / 3 cl fresh lemon juice
0.3 oz / 1 cl pineapple syrup

•

GARNISH

Seasonal fruits

PREPARATION

Shake in a shaker over ice for about 10 seconds and strain into a glass over crushed ice. Garnish with seasonal fruit.

•

Glass: highball glass

1909

Carl A. Seutter, The Mixologist

———

Harvard

↓

2 oz / 6 cl Hennessy Cognac or brandy
1 oz / 3 cl red vermouth
2 dashes The Bitter Truth Orange Bitters

•

GARNISH

Lemon zest

•

PREPARATION

Stir gently in a mixing glass over ice for about 10 seconds, then strain into a glass. Garnish with a lemon twist.

•

Glass: martini glass

1935

A. S. Crockett, The Old Waldorf-Astoria Bar Book

———

Jack Rose

↓

2 oz / 6 cl applejack brandy

1 oz / 3 cl fresh lemon juice
0.7 oz / 2 cl grenadine

•

GARNISH

None

•

PREPARATION

Shake vigorously in a shaker over ice for about 10 seconds and strain into the glass.

•

Glass:cocktail coupe

1905

Frank J. May, The National Police Gazette

———

Japanese Cocktail

↓

2 oz / 6 cl Hennessy Cognac or brandy
0.5 oz / 1.5 cl almond syrup
4 dashes The Bitter Truth Jerry Thomas Bitters

•

GARNISH

Lemon zest

•

PREPARATION

Stir gently in a mixing glass over ice for about 10 seconds, then strain into a glass. Garnish with a lemon twist.

•

Glass: cocktail coupe

1887

Jerry Thomas, The Bon Vivant's Companion

Prince of Wales Original

2.7 oz / 8 cl Madeira

0.3 oz / 1 cl orange curaçao

0.2 oz / 0.5 cl nut liqueur

1 bs powdered sugar

•

TOPPING

3.4 oz / 10 cl Moët & Chandon Brut Champagne

Cherry liqueur

•

GARNISH

Lemon zest

•

PREPARATION

Stir gently in a mixing glass over ice for about 10 seconds and strain into a champagne glass over crushed ice. Top up with champagne and float with cherry liqueur. Garnish with a lemon twist.

•

Glass: champagne glass

Louis Fouquet, Bariana

———

Prince of Wales

(The Ritz)

0.7 oz / 2 cl Hennessy Cognac

0.7 oz / 2 cl Madeira

2 dashes The Bitter Truth Aromatic Bitters

0.2 oz / 0.5 cl orange curaçao

TOPPING

4 oz / 12 cl Moët & Chandon Brut Champagne

•

GARNISH

Orange zest

•

PREPARATION

Shake vigorously in a shaker over ice for about 10 seconds and top with champagne. Garnish with orange zest.

•

Glass: champagne glass

Frank Meier, The Artistry of Mixing Drinks

———

Sazerac

2 dashes absinthe

2 oz / 6 cl Hennessy Cognac

1 sugar cube (alternative: 0.3 oz / 1 cl sugar syrup, see page 222)

6 dashes Peychaud's Bitters (alternative: The Bitter Truth Creole Bitters)

•

GARNISH

Lemon zest

•

PREPARATION

Rinse the tumbler with absinthe. Stir cognac, sugar and bitters gently in a mixing glass for about 10 seconds and strain into a glass without ice. Garnish with a lemon twist.

•

Glass: tumbler—Old Fashioned glass

John Schiller, "The Sazerac Coffee House," New Orleans

———

Sidecar

1 oz / 3 cl Hennessy Cognac (I recommend 2 oz / 6 cl Cognac)

1 oz / 3 cl fresh lemon juice

1 oz / 3 cl triple sec

•

GARNISH

Lemon zest

•

PREPARATION

Shake vigorously in a shaker over ice for about 10 seconds and strain into a glass. Garnish with a lemon twist.

•

Glass: cocktail coupe

Harry MacElhone, Barflies and Cocktails

———

Soyer au Champagne

0.3 oz / 1 cl cognac

0.3 oz / 1 cl orange curaçao

0.3 oz / 1 cl Maraschino

2 bs vanilla ice cream

1 oz / 3 cl Hennessy Cognac

0.7 oz / 2 cl sugar syrup (see page 222)

1.5 oz / 4.5 cl whole milk (3.5%)

•

TOPPING

Champagne

•

GARNISH

Orange zest

Small pineapple cubes

•

PREPARATION

Stir gently in the cocktail glass and top up with champagne. Garnish with orange zest and pineapple cubes.

•

Glass: cocktail coupe

1927

Harry MacElhone, Barflies and Cocktails

———

Stinger

2 oz / 6 cl Hennessy Cognac

0.7 oz / 2 cl crème de menthe blanche

•

GARNISH

Mint leaf

•

PREPARATION

Stir gently in a mixing glass over ice for about 10 seconds, then strain into a glass. Garnish with a mint leaf.

•

Glass: martini glass

1930

Harry Craddock, The Savoy Cocktail Book
"American Bar," Savoy Hotel, London

———

The Bombay Cocktail

1.7 oz / 5 cl Hennessy Cognac

0.5 oz / 1.5 cl dry vermouth

0.5 oz / 1.5 cl red vermouth

0.3 oz / 1 cl orange curaçao

0.2 oz / 0.5 cl absinthe

•

GARNISH

Lemon zest

•

PREPARATION

Stir gently in a mixing glass over ice for about 10 seconds, then strain into a glass. Garnish with a lemon twist.

•

Glass: cocktail coupe

1930

Harry Craddock, The Savoy Cocktail Book
"American Bar," Savoy Hotel, London

Sake & Shōchū Cocktails

I could fill whole chapters with these two drinks, because in my view, sake and shōchū are some of the most important and complex spirits out there. Although both come from Japan, the main difference is how they are made: Shōchū is distilled, while sake is fermented. Sake production was originally the preserve of the imperial court and was only later passed on to selected monasteries. The quality of the final product depended on the quality of its basic ingredients, including water, rice, and yeast. The key factors affecting the taste are mainly the degree of polishing of the rice and the hardness of the water. If sake isn't being drunk cold or warm from special cups or wooden cubes, you'll find it used in Japanese cooking. Even though its production method originated in Korea and China, shōchū is actually native to the Japanese port city of Kagoshima. Barley, sweet potato, sugar cane, or rice are used as the base ingredients for the distillate. This "Japanese vodka," as it is sometimes called, has a much higher alcohol content than sake. There are taste differences too: shōchū is less fruity than sake, so is better for cocktails than for drinking straight.

Damn It, Jimmy

1.5 oz / 4.5 cl sake
1.5 oz / 4.5 cl white rum
0.3 oz / 0.75 cl fino sherry
0.3 oz / 0.75 cl dry vermouth
0.2 oz / 0.5 cl sugar syrup (see page 222)

•

GARNISH
Green olive stuffed with blue cheese

•

PREPARATION
Stir gently in a mixing glass over ice for about 10 seconds, then strain into a glass. Garnish with an olive.

•

Glass: martini glass

Simon Difford, "The Cabinet Room," London

Japonais 75

1.4 oz / 4 cl Shochu
0.3 oz / 0.75 cl sugar syrup (see page 222)
5 oz / 15 cl ginger ale

•

GARNISH
Long lemon twist

PREPARATION
Stir gently in a champagne glass. Garnish with a lemon twist.

•

Glass: champagne glass

Koku Sour

2 oz / 6 cl shōchū
1 oz / 3 cl fresh lemon juice
0.7 oz / 2 cl sugar syrup (see page 222)

•

GARNISH
Lemon zest
Maraschino cherry

•

PREPARATION
Shake well in a shaker over ice for about 10 seconds, then strain into a glass. Garnish with lemon zest and a maraschino cherry.

•

Glass: tumbler—Old Fashioned glass

Lychee Sake Martini

2 oz / 6 cl sake
1.5 oz / 4.5 cl Belvedere Vodka

1 oz / 3 cl lychee syrup (from the can)
2 lychees (canned)

GARNISH

1 Lychee

PREPARATION

Shake vigorously in a shaker over ice for about 10 seconds and strain into a glass. Garnish with lychee.

Glass: cocktail coupe

MT. Fuji

2 oz / 6 cl Shochu
0.7 oz / 2 cl fresh lemon juice
0.5 oz / 1.5 cl sugar syrup (see page 222)
0.7 oz / 2 cl pomegranate juice
2 basil leaves

GARNISH

Apple slice

PREPARATION

Shake vigorously in a shaker over ice for about 10 seconds and strain into a glass. Garnish with an apple slice.

Glass: martini glass

Old Fashioned Samurai

2 oz / 6 cl sake
0.3 oz / 1 cl sugar syrup (see page 222)
4 dashes The Bitter Truth Orange Bitters

GARNISH

Orange zest

Lemon zest

Maraschino cherry

PREPARATION

Stir gently in a mixing glass over ice for about 10 seconds, then strain into a glass. Garnish with zest and a maraschino cherry.

Glass: tumbler—Old Fashioned glass

Sake Martini

2 oz / 6 cl sake
2 oz / 6 cl Tanqueray No. TEN Gin
1.4 oz / 4 cl dry vermouth

GARNISH

Apple slice

PREPARATION

Stir gently in a mixing glass over ice for about 10 seconds, then strain into a glass. Garnish with an apple slice.

Glass: martini glass

Tokyo Mule

2 oz / 6 cl Shochu
0.3 oz / 1 cl fresh lime juice
5 oz / 15 cl ginger beer (see page 148)

GARNISH

Lime zest

PREPARATION

Stir gently in a highball glass. Garnish with lime zest.

Glass: highball glass or copper mug

Pisco & Cachaça Cocktails

Pisco is also known as „the brandy of Latin America." Opinions are divided as who actually invented it, with Peru and Chile each claiming the title for themselves. In fact, their two versions are quite different from each other. Chilean pisco is distilled from various sweet grape varieties and has a short resting period before being diluted with water to drinking strength. Peruvian pisco is known for its greater elegance. The only ingredient common to both drinks is fermented grape must. Where mixing is concerned, both Chilean and Peruvian pisco are easy to handle; it's best if the bartender is guided by the guest's wishes.

Who doesn't know the world-famous Caipirinha, so popular here on hot days, which all bartenders can mix in their sleep? The main ingredient is cachaça, a Brazilian spirit made from sugarcane juice by about 6,000 specialist companies including many small farms; many of those products are only sold in Brazil. As with cognac, there are quality differences when it comes to cachaça; like a long-aged cognac, well-aged cachaças can fetch high prices. But until this trend takes off in Europe, cachaça will continue its life as a cocktail ingredient.

Caipirinha

2 oz / 6 cl Cachaça
1 lime
3 bs white cane sugar or
0.7 oz / 2 cl sugar syrup (see page 222)

•

GARNISH
None

•

PREPARATION
Shake well in a shaker over ice for about 10 seconds, then strain into a glass.

•

Glass: tumbler—Old Fashioned glass

Brazil's national drink

Pisco Punch

2 oz / 6 cl pisco
1 oz / 3 cl fresh lemon juice
0.7 oz / 2 cl pineapple syrup

•

GARNISH
Small pineapple cubes

PREPARATION
Shake well in a shaker over ice for about 10 seconds, then strain into a glass. Garnish with pineapple cubes.

•

Glass: sour glass

Duncan Nicol, San Francisco

Pisco Sour

2 oz / 6 cl Pisco
1 oz / 3 cl fresh lemon juice
0.7 oz / 2 cl sugar syrup (see page 222)
1 egg white

•

TOPPING
3 dashes The Bitter Truth Aromatic Bitters

•

GARNISH
None

•

PREPARATION
Shake vigorously in a shaker over ice for about 10 seconds, then add bitters on top of the foam.

•

Glass: sour glass

National drink of Chile and Peru

Champagne Cocktails

The French sparkling wine is one of my favorite drinks, and I love to enjoy it every now and then. And it's always there to refresh me, not just on hot summer days. There are a few sparkling wines out there—but only those made in the Champagne region using the "méthode champenoise" can actually be called Champagne. It's used in all sorts of mixed drinks, but keep in mind: the cocktail should be made in the same amount of time it takes to pour a glass of Champagne. If you're topping the drink with Champagne, don't add too many flavors—let the Champagne and the cocktail shine on their own. We think a Champagne cocktail should not countenance substitutes like prosecco, cava, or crémant. Because Champagne is the king of sparkling wines, and that's the standard every bartender should aim for.

Air Mail

1 oz / 3 cl white rum
0.5 oz / 1.5 cl fresh lime juice
0.5 oz / 1.5 cl honey syrup (see page 221)

•

TOPPING
3.4 oz / 10 cl Moët & Chandon Brut Champagne

•

GARNISH
None

•

PREPARATION
Shake vigorously in a shaker over ice for about 10 seconds, strain into a champagne glass and top with champagne.

•

Glass: champagne glass

1941

W. C. Whitfield, Here's How

Bellini

1.7 oz / 5 cl white peach purée
(ideally white vineyard peach)
4 oz / 12 cl Moët & Chandon Brut Champagne

GARNISH
None

•

PREPARATION
Stir gently in a champagne glass.

•

Glass: champagne glass

1948

Guiseppe Cipriani, "Harry's Bar," Venice

Black Velvet

1.7 oz / 5 cl Guinness
3.4 oz / 10 cl Moët & Chandon Brut Champagne

•

GARNISH
None

•

PREPARATION
Stir gently in the glass.

•

Glass: champagne glass

1861

"Brooks's Club," London

Buck's Fizz

1.7 oz / 5 cl fresh orange juice
4 oz / 12 cl Moët & Chandon Brut Champagne

•

GARNISH
None

•

PREPARATION
Stir gently in a champagne glass.

•

Glass: champagne glass

1930

Harry Craddock, The Savoy Cocktail Book
"American Bar," Savoy Hotel, London

Champagne Julep

3.4 oz / 10 cl Moët & Chandon Brut Champagne
0.3 oz / 1 cl sugar syrup (see page 222)
10 mint leaves

•

TOPPING
0.3 oz / 1 cl Hennessy Cognac

•

GARNISH
Mint sprig

•

PREPARATION
Pour sugar syrup over mint leaves in the cup
and muddle them. Add champagne, fill up
with crushed ice and stir. Top with cognac

and garnish with a mint sprig.

•

Glass: julep cup

Champagne Punch

FOR 4–6 PEOPLE
2 oranges
10 fresh strawberries
½ pineapple
Leaves from 10 mint sprigs
1.7 oz / 5 cl Hennessy Cognac
1.7 oz / 5 cl Cointreau
17 oz / 50 cl soda water
1 bottle Moët & Chandon Brut Champagne

•

GARNISH
None

•

PREPARATION
Cut 6 zest strips from one orange; slice the
second orange into nice rounds. Halve the
strawberries, cut the pineapple into pieces.
Put all ingredients including ice into a bowl
and stir gently.

•

Glass: cup

Champagne Cocktail

1 sugar cube
2 dashes The Bitter Truth Aromatic Bitters
3.4 oz / 10 cl Moët & Chandon Brut Champagne

•

GARNISH
Lemon zest

•

PREPARATION
Stir gently in a champagne glass.
Garnish with a lemon twist.

•

Glass: champagne glass

1862

Jerry Thomas, The Bar-Tender's Guide

Death in the Afternoon

1.4 oz / 4 cl absinthe
4 oz / 12 cl Moët & Chandon Brut Champagne

•

GARNISH
None

•

PREPARATION
Stir gently in a champagne glass.

•

Glass: champagne glass

1935

Ernest Hemingway,
So Red the Nose or Breath in the Afternoon

French 75

↓

1 oz / 3 cl Tanqueray No. TEN Gin
0.5 oz / 1.5 cl fresh lemon juice
0.3 oz / 1 cl sugar syrup (see page 222)

•

TOPPING
3.4 oz / 10 cl Moët & Chandon Brut Champagne

•

GARNISH
Lemon zest

•

PREPARATION
Shake vigorously in a shaker over ice for
about 10 seconds, then top with champagne.
Garnish with lemon zest.

•

Glass: champagne glass

1930

Harry Craddock, The Savoy Cocktail Book
"American Bar," Savoy Hotel, London

James Bond

↓

1 sugar cube
2 dashes The Bitter Truth Aromatic Bitters
1 oz / 3 cl Belvedere Vodka

TOPPING
3.4 oz / 10 cl Moët & Chandon Brut Champagne

•

GARNISH
None

•

PREPARATION
Stir gently in a champagne glass.

•

Glass: Champagne glass

Jubal Early Punch

↓

0.7 oz / 2 cl Hennessy Cognac
0.7 oz / 2 cl Bulleit Bourbon Whiskey
0.5 oz / 1.5 cl fresh lemon juice
0.5 oz / 1.5 cl sugar syrup (see page 222)
0.7 oz / 2 cl still water
3.4 oz / 10 cl Moët & Chandon Brut Champagne

•

GARNISH
None

•

PREPARATION
Stir gently in a large cup.

•

Glass: cup

Kir Royal

↓

0.3 oz / 1 cl crème de cassis
4 oz / 12 cl Moët & Chandon Brut Champagne

GARNISH
None

•

PREPARATION
Stir gently in a champagne glass.

•

Glass: champagne glass

Felix Kir, France

Mimosa

↓

3.4 oz / 10 cl fresh orange juice
1.7 oz / 5 cl Moët & Chandon Brut Champagne

•

GARNISH
None

•

PREPARATION
Stir gently in a champagne glass.

•

Glass: champagne glass

1930

Harry Craddock, The Savoy Cocktail Book
"American Bar," Savoy Hotel, London

Negroni Sbagliato

↓

1 oz / 3 cl Campari and 1 oz / 3 cl red vermouth
2 oz / 6 cl Moët & Chandon Brut Champagne

GARNISH

Orange zest

•

PREPARATION

Stir gently in the tumbler. Garnish
with orange zest.

•

Glass: tumbler—Old Fashioned glass

"Bar Basso," Milan

Ohio

0.7 oz / 2 cl Bulleit Rye Whiskey
0.7 oz / 2 cl red vermouth
0.2 oz / 0.5 cl triple sec
2 dashes The Bitter Truth Aromatic Bitters
3.4 oz / 10 cl Moët & Chandon Brut Champagne

GARNISH

None

•

PREPARATION

Stir gently in a mixing glass over ice for about
10 seconds, strain into a champagne glass and
top with champagne.

•

Glass: champagne glass

Pick me up

1 oz / 3 cl Hennessy Cognac
0.3 oz / 1 cl fresh lemon juice
0.2 oz / 0.5 cl sugar syrup (see page 222)
0.2 oz / 0.5 cl grenadine

1 dash The Bitter Truth Aromatic Bitters

•

TOPPING

3.4 oz / 10 cl Moët & Chandon Brut Champagne

•

GARNISH

None

•

PREPARATION

Shake vigorously in a shaker over ice for
about 10 seconds, strain into a champagne
glass and top with champagne.

•

Glass: champagne glass

Ritz

0.7 oz / 2 cl Hennessy Cognac
0.7 oz / 2 cl fresh orange juice
0.3 oz / 1 cl Cointreau

•

TOPPING

3.4 / 10 cl Moët & Chandon Brut Champagne

•

GARNISH

None

•

PREPARATION

Shake vigorously in a shaker over ice for
about 10 seconds, strain into a champagne
glass and top with champagne.

•

Glass: champagne glass

Ritz Hotels

Seelbach Cocktail

1 oz / 3 cl Bulleit Bourbon whiskey
0.5 oz / 1.5 cl Cointreau
6 dashes The Bitter Truth Aromatic Bitters
6 dashes Peychaud's Bitters or
The Bitter Truth Creole Bitters

•

GARNISH

Orange zest

•

PREPARATION

Stir gently in a champagne glass.
Garnish with orange zest.

•

Glass: champagne glass

"Seelbach Hotel," Louisville

The Champagne Flamingo

0.7 oz / 2 cl Belvedere Vodka
0.7 oz / 2 cl Campari
4 oz / 12 cl Moët & Chandon Brut Champagne

GARNISH

Lemon zest

•

PREPARATION

Stir gently in a champagne glass.
Garnish with a lemon twist.

•

Glass: champagne glass

Liqueur Cocktails

Liqueurs are aromatic alcoholic spirits with an extremely high sugar content. They've been used in medicine and enjoyed as a treat since the 13th century. Current EU regulations say that every liter of liqueur has to have 100 grams of sugar. For cocktails, we use liqueurs less as a base and more as so-called "flavouring agents"—basically, to add aroma. All those different colors come from natural or industrial dyes added to the product. The forerunners of today's liqueurs were the aromatic wines of the Ancient Greeks and Romans. Bols, De Kuyper, and Marie Brizard are the oldest liqueur makers and also the commonest brands you'll find in bars. But the absolute favorite among bartenders is Chartreuse, which is still produced in monasteries.

Aperol Spritz

1.4 oz / 4 cl Aperol
2 oz / 6 cl prosecco
0.7 oz / 2 cl soda water

•

GARNISH
1 Orange slice

•

PREPARATION
Pour into a wine glass over ice and stir gently. Garnish with an orange slice.

•

Glass: wine glass

From Northern Italy

Pharmacy

1 oz / 3 cl Fernet Branca
1 oz / 3 cl Punt e Mes
0.7 oz / 2 cl crème de menthe verte
1 dash The Bitter Truth Aromatic Bitters

•

GARNISH
None

•

PREPARATION
Stir gently in a mixing glass over ice for about 10 seconds, then strain into a glass.

Glass: martini glass

Grasshopper

1 oz / 3 cl crème de menthe verte
1 oz / 3 cl white crème de cacao
1.4 oz / 4 cl cream

•

GARNISH
Mint leaf

•

PREPARATION
Shake well in a shaker over ice for about 10 seconds, then strain into a glass. Garnish with a mint leaf.

•

Glass: martini glass

Philibert Guichet, "Tujaque's Bar," New Orleans

Pimm's No. 1 Cup

1.7 oz / 5 cl Pimm's No. 1
5 oz / 15 cl lemon soda
Cucumber peel

GARNISH
Seasonal fruits
Cucumber peel

•

PREPARATION
Stir gently in a highball glass. Add cucumber
peel and garnish with seasonal fruits and
cucumber peel.

•

Glass: highball glass

1823

James Pimm, "Pimm's Oyster Bar," London

Prairie Oyster

2 bs ketchup
6 dashes Worcestershire sauce
0.2 oz / 0.5 cl fresh lemon juice
2 dashes Tabasco
1 pinch salt and 1 pinch pepper
1 egg yolk

•

GARNISH
None

•

PREPARATION
Mix all the ingredients except the egg
yolk together in a mixing glass. Pour into a
martini glass, add the egg yolk, and drink it
down in one.

•

Glass: martini glass

1930

*Harry Craddock, The Savoy Cocktail Book
"American Bar," Savoy Hotel, London*

Cihan's 50 Best Original Creations

In this chapter, you'll find my own creations, which I'm publishing here for the very first time. I often kept my methods and measurements secret, but now I think it's time to share my knowledge and recipes. The special thing about my old bar "Circle" was that the cocktails didn't have fancy names—they were just numbered to make ordering evasier for guests. Because for me, what's more important than any title are the cocktails themselves, their taste, and their ingredients—that's what I focus on. I'm really happy to share the knowledge I've picked up on the next pages, and I hope everyone can mix these cocktails at home.

Cocktail No. 1

TEATIME IN KYOTO

This drink is my tribute to Japan. During my many trips to this amazing country, especially in 2015 in Kyoto and Kobe, the idea for this cocktail came to me. During a tea ceremony in Kyoto, I thought of a matcha tea syrup, and in one of the best steakhouses in Kobe, the fat just melted in my mouth—that's when I thought of the whiskey infusion with Kobe beef fat.

2 oz / 6 cl Bulleit Rye Whiskey, infused with
Kobe beef fat (see right)

0.3 oz / 1 cl matcha syrup (see page 222)

2–3 dashes The Bitter Truth Orange Bitters

•

GARNISH

Lemon peel

Dehydrated lemon slice

•

PREPARATION

Stir gently in a mixing glass over ice for
about 10 seconds, then strain into the glass.
Squeeze lemon peel over the drink and add a
dehydrated lemon slice to the glass.

•

Glass: tumbler—Old Fashioned glass

**BULLEIT RYE WHISKEY INFUSION
WITH KOBE BEEF FAT**

*For the fat-washing method, prepare a ratio of **50 g fat to 1 l whiskey (1.8 oz fat to 34 oz whiskey)**. Melt the fat in a pan or in the oven, making sure it doesn't get too hot. Pour the whiskey into a sealable container and add the melted, warm fat. Seal the container tightly, shake it, and put it in the freezer so the fat rises to the top. Strain through a sieve or similar filter and pour the liquid back into the original bottle.*

Cocktail No. 2

AND THE OSCAR GOES TO … AMERIQUE CHERIE

I mixed this cocktail in 2013 at the Global Finals of the Bacardi Grey Goose World Competition in Cognac, France. 15 countries qualified for it, and I managed to win for Germany and brought the trophy home. This drink was chosen as the official cocktail of the 2014 Academy Awards—that is, the Oscars in Los Angeles.

6 green seedless grapes
(preferably from the Cognac region)

1 tsp dried lavender

2 oz / 6 cl Grey Goose Vodka

1 oz / 3 cl fresh lime juice

0.7 oz / 2 cl honey syrup with wheat and
bitters (see page 221)

•

GARNISH

Lime zest

2 grapes

Lavender sprig

•

PREPARATION

Gently crush the grapes and lavender, add all
the other ingredients, and shake hard over
ice in a shaker for about 10 seconds. Strain
through a double strainer and garnish with lime
zest, grapes, and a sprig of lavender.

•

Glass: tumbler—Old Fashioned glass

DRY VERMOUTH INFUSION
WITH SHISO
Put 1 l (34 oz) dry vermouth and 10 shiso leaves
in a large sealable container, let it infuse for 1
week at room temperature, and make sure the
shiso leaves do not start to wilt. Strain through a
simple filter and pour into a clean bottle.

Cocktail No. 3

ROOTS FROM JAPAN

For this cocktail, I was mainly inspired by roots and mushrooms. I especially love the smell of morels because it reminds me of a dish I ate when I was younger. The morels go perfectly with truffles, which we bring together in this drink. By combining high-quality eau de vie from a German distillery, sake, and shiso leaf, we're also giving a little nod to Japan.

2 oz / 6 cl sake, infused with morels
(see right)

0.3 oz / 1 cl Stählemühle Black Truffle
Eau de Vie

0.7 oz / 2 cl dry vermouth, infused
with shiso leaves (see page 70)

•

GARNISH
Pandan leaves

•

PREPARATION
Stir gently in a mixing glass over ice for about
10 seconds, then strain into a glass.
Garnish with pandan leaves.

•

Glass: cocktail coupe

SAKE-MOREL-INFUSION
Let 1 l (34 oz) sake and 25 g (0.8 oz) dried morels infuse sous-vide at in a water bath at 58 degrees for about 3 hours. Then take it out and chill. Filter through a coffee filter and pour into a clean bottle.

Cocktail No. 4

COFFEE, CHOCOLATE, CHESTNUTS

Coffee and chestnuts inspired me to make this outstanding cocktail. Coffee, because my daily espresso at the Italian café bar has become part of my routine—the only alternative for me is a good filter coffee, which I've also come to enjoy. Whenever I smell roasted coffee beans, I always think of the roasted chestnuts my mom used to make for me and my siblings, so I got the idea to combine these two flavors.

2 oz / 6 cl sake–vodka infusion with Kenyan coffee and muscovado sugar (see right)
0.3 oz / 1 cl Amaro Nonino
2 dashes The Bitter Truth Chocolate Bitters

•

TOPPING
Chestnut cream

•

GARNISH
Dried chestnuts

•

PREPARATION
Stir gently in a mixing glass over ice for about 10 seconds, strain into a glass, and top with chestnut cream. Chop up dried chestnuts and sprinkle them on top.

•

Glass: cocktail coupe

SAKE-VODKA INFUSION WITH KENYAN COFFEE AND MUSCOVADO SUGAR

Mix 2 l (68 oz) sake and 500 ml (17 oz) vodka in a sealable container with 200 g (7.1 oz) Kenyan coffee beans. After 3 days, add 100 g (3.5 oz) muscovado sugar and let it infuse for another 2 days, stirring once after 24 hours.

Cocktail No. 5

KENTUCKY – MUCH LOVE

A Halloween cocktail with pumpkin—bourbon is just the perfect match for it. I got the idea for this combo after someone asked me to create a Halloween cocktail for a special event. This was supposed to be more of a "guy's drink," a bit stronger in flavor and with a dominant spirit. The mix worked right away, and a fantastic, aromatic drink was born—one that makes you want more than just one.

2 oz / 6 cl Michter's Bourbon Whiskey,
infused with pumpkin (see right)
0.3 oz / 1 cl Ancho Reyes
2 bs maple syrup
2 dashes The Bitter Truth Aromatic Bitters

•

GARNISH
Dried apple slice

•

PREPARATION
Stir gently in a mixing glass over ice for about
10 seconds, then strain into a glass.
Garnish with a dried apple slice.

•

Glass: tumbler—Old Fashioned glass

**MICHTER'S BOURBON
WHISKEY INFUSION WITH PUMPKIN**

*Cut 200 g (7.1 oz) pumpkin into cubes and roast in the oven at 80°C/175°F top heat for 1 hour. Once the pumpkin is nicely roasted, take it out and let it cool to lukewarm. **Infuse 1 l (34 oz) Michter's Bourbon Whiskey** with the roasted pumpkin in a sous-vide water bath at 58°C/136°F for 2 hours. Then take it out and chill. Just filter it and pour into a clean bottle.*

Cocktail No. 6

KNOCK KNOCK, WHO'S THERE?

This cocktail is rather an eggnog with egg and milk, but the mezcal brings in a spirit that's very trendy with bartenders right now. Mezcal Tobala is a high-quality, premium agave spirit, and in this combo, its flavors really shine. The togarashi-spiced sugar syrup gives the cocktail an exotic touch, and the almond milk—which you can find in any well-stocked organic or regular supermarket rounds off the drink perfectly.

1 oz / 3 cl mezcal tobalá
0.7 oz / 2 cl fino sherry
1 oz / 3 cl almond milk
0.5 oz / 1.5 cl togarashi syrup (see page 222)
1 egg

•

GARNISH
1 Pinch of togarashi

•

PREPARATION
Shake well in a shaker over ice for about 10 seconds, then strain into a glass. Dust with togarashi.

•

Glass: sour glass

Cocktail No. 7

AQUA, AQUA, VIT

Aquavit is known as an aromatic digestif that's usually served ice-cold, (but should not be stored in the freezer). It's been making a comeback for a while now, not least because it's perfect for cocktails. This trend—although I hesitate to use the word, since trends are always fleeting—came to us from the Nordic countries and has been winning over both guests and bartenders here in Germany. For this cocktail, we went with a fruity version that could easily be called a Sour. With the fresh juices and ginger, which adds a nice balanced kick, this drink is a treat any time of year.

2 slices ginger, freshly cut
1.7 oz / 5 cl Linie Aquavit
0.7 oz / 2 cl fino sherry
0.7 oz / 2 cl fresh carrot juice
0.8 oz / 2.5 cl fresh lemon juice
0.5 oz / 1.5 cl honey syrup (see page 221)
1 egg white

•

GARNISH
Thyme sprig

•

PREPARATION
Muddle the sliced ginger in the shaker, add
the other ingredients over ice, and shake hard
for about 10 seconds. Strain into a glass and
garnish with a thyme sprig.

•

Glass: tumbler—Old Fashioned glass

Cocktail No. 8

SWEET, STRONG, SOUR

This cocktail brings together a host of different elements, but they all work together beautifully. The ginger syrup and ginger beer add a gentle heat, the tequila gives it a nice kick, and the fresh juices help give the drink that extra zing.

1.4 oz / 4 cl Don Julio Blanco Tequila
0.3 oz / 1 cl Stählemühle Blood Orange
0.7 oz / 2 cl fresh carrot juice
0.8 oz / 2.5 cl fresh lime juice
0.5 oz / 1.5 cl ginger syrup (see page 221)

•

TOPPING
8 cl Ginger beer (see page 148)

•

GARNISH
Thinly sliced carrot sticks

•

PREPARATION
Shake in a shaker over ice for about 10 seconds, strain into a glass, and top with ginger beer. Add the carrot sticks on top.

•

Glass: highball glass

Cocktail No. 9

JAPANESE CEREMONY

Sweet potato, chocolate, matcha tea, yuzu, and gin may sound like a weird combo at first, but this cocktail brings all the flavors together into a real explosion of taste. You can taste every single component, and this cocktail hits all the senses from the very first sip. A drink for the pros, but even beginners will end up loving it.

2 oz / 6 cl Tanqueray No. TEN Gin, infused
with sweet potatoes (see right)

0.3 oz / 0.75 cl matcha syrup (see page 222)

1 dash The Bitter Truth Chocolate Bitters

0.3 oz / 1 cl yuzu liqueur

•

GARNISH
Edible flowers

•

PREPARATION

Stir gently in a mixing glass over ice for about
10 seconds, then strain into a glass.
Garnish with edible flowers.

•

Glass: tumbler—Old Fashioned glass

**TANQUERAY No. TEN GIN INFUSION
WITH SWEET POTATO**

Dice 200 g (7.1 oz) sweet potatoes and bake at 120°C/ /250°F top heat for 1 hour. Once the sweet potatoes are nicely roasted, take them out and let them cool to lukewarm. Infuse 1 l (34 oz) gin with the roasted potatoes in a sous-vide water bath for 3 hours at 60°C/140°F. Then take it out and chill. Just filter it and pour into a clean bottle.

Cocktail No. TEN

THAT DRINK MAKES YOU ...

This cocktail is a twist on the classic Negroni. Here we're using mezcal again, which gives the drink a smoky note, and Pussanga—,a spirit made in Germany that's known for its gentle heat and—don't say we didn't warn you—its aphrodisiac effect. Barolo Chinato from Cocchi makes a great vermouth for this, and a little touch of vanilla finishes the cocktail off perfectly.

1 oz / 3 cl mezcal tobalá
0.7 oz / 2 cl Pussanga
0.7 oz / 2 cl Cocchi Vermouth Barolo Chinato
1 bs Stählemühle Vanilla Eau de Vie
2 dashes Peychaud's Bitters or
The Bitter Truth Creole Bitters

•

TOPPING
Orange zest

•

GARNISH
Dried chestnuts

•

PREPARATION
Stir gently in a mixing glass over ice for about
10 seconds, then strain into a glass.
Garnish with orange zest.

•

Glass: tumbler—Old Fashioned glass

BAROLO CHINATO
*The **Barolo wine** is enhanced with red cinchona root, cinchona bark, rhubarb root, ginseng root, gentian, cardamom seeds, and a host of other spices and herbs. This flavored wine is then aged in oak barrels.*

PUSSANGA

This fruity premium spirit with a subtle kick and a hint of bitterness is made from the aphrodisiac South American pussanga plants, plus pomegranate, chili, ginger, and cardamom.

Cocktail No. 11

WALKING IN THE FOREST

The forest plays a big part in this cocktail. While I was out jogging in the morning, I was struck by the distinctive fragrance of the trees, and felt compelled to capture it in a cocktail. The mist created here with dry ice creates a cool effect and shows that serving a cocktail is all about attention to detail.

1.7 oz / 5 cl Tanqueray No. TEN Gin, infused
with porcini mushrooms (see right)

0.7 oz / 2 cl Cocchi Vermouth Barolo Chinato

2 dashes eucalyptus bitters

•

GARNISH

Lemon zest

•

PREPARATION

Stir gently in a mixing glass over ice for about
10 seconds, then strain into a glass.
Garnish with a lemon twist.

•

Glass: cocktail coupe

**TANQUERAY No. TEN GIN
INFUSION WITH PORCINI
MUSHROOMS**

Infuse 200 g (7.1 oz) dried porcini mushrooms and 1 l (34 oz) gin isous-vide in a water bath at 60 degrees for 3 hours. Remove and chill. Filter and pour into a clean bottle.

Cocktail No. 12

NO RED, GO AHEAD

This drink is a fruity, aromatic whiskey-based cocktail that mixes sherry, Suze, and coriander. The best part: It's not just refreshing, it also makes an awesome aperitif.

1 oz / 3 cl Bulleit Rye Whiskey
0.7 oz / 2 cl oloroso sherry
0.5 oz / 1.5 cl fresh lemon juice
0.3 oz / 1 cl coriander syrup (see page 222)
0.2 oz / 0.5 cl Suze
1 dash Dr. Adam Elmegirab's Aphrodite Bitters
2 coffee beans

•

GARNISH
3 Coffee beans

•

PREPARATION

Crush the coffee beans in the shaker with a muddler. Add all the other ingredients and shake hard over ice for about 10 seconds. Strain into a glass and garnish with coffee beans.

•

Glass: cocktail coupe

OLOROSO SHERRY

An oloroso sherry undergoes oxidative aging and is usually more complex and aromatic than a fino or amontillado sherry. It typically has a nutty aroma and usually contains 17 to 20 percent alcohol.

SUZE

Suze is a gentian liqueur with a bittersweet
taste, distilled from the roots of yellow gentian.
It's popular as an aperitif, but is also great in
cocktails.

Cocktail No. 13

FROM #RETHINKTHEWORLD

*This cocktail was one of the most popular drinks at my bar "Circle."
That's because of its combination of rum and cigar, which makes it a real treat
for any cigar or smoking aficionados. As you will find, making it isn't nearly as
complicated as it looks at first glance.*

1 cigar leaf
2 oz / 6 cl Bacardi 8 Rum
1 oz / 3 cl fresh lemon juice
0.7 oz / 2 cl honey syrup (see page 221)
0.5 oz / 1.5 cl cigar syrup (see page 222)
3 dashes Fee Brothers Plum Bitters

•

GARNISH
3 Stemmed cherries

•

PREPARATION
Break up the cigar leaf and place it on a
fireproof surface. Light it and immediately
cover with the tumbler so the smoke is trapped
and the glass gets "smoked." Shake all the
other ingredients over ice in a shaker for about
10 seconds and strain into the glass. Garnish
with stemmed cherries.

•

Glass: tumbler—Old Fashioned glass

Cocktail No. 14

COCONUT MEXICAN MARTINI

You might think this is just a sweet mezcal martini with coconut foam, but the drink is far more complex than you'd expect. The caramelized coconut flakes, the mezcal with all its nuances,, the sweet vanilla, the dry shiso vermouth—the mix of all these ingredients makes it clear from the very first sip that this cocktail is anything but simple. Because of its kick, it's also proven to be an exciting companion to a sweet dessert.

1.2 oz / 3.5 cl Mezcal Tobalá
0.8 oz / 2.5 cl dry vermouth, infused with
shiso leaves (see right)
0.3 oz / 1 cl vanilla syrup (see page 222)
2 dashes Dr. Adam Elmegirab's Teapot Bitters

•

TOPPING
Coconut espuma (see page 222)

•

GARNISH
Sugar syrup (see page 222)
1 bs Coconut flakes

•

PREPARATION
Moisten the rim of the glass with sugar syrup
and sprinkle with coconut flakes. Stir the
ingredients gently in a mixing glass over ice
for about 10 seconds, strain into the glass,
and top with coconut espuma. Sprinkle
coconut flakes on top and caramelize briefly.

•

Glass: cocktail coupe

**DRY VERMOUTH INFUSION
WITH SHISO**

Place 1 l (34 oz) dry vermouth and 10 shiso leaves in a large sealable container and infuse for 1 week. Make sure the shiso leaves do not start to wilt. Then filter through a simple filter and pour into a clean bottle.

Cocktail No. 15

SEA, I SEE THE SEA

A fruity cocktail that would fit right into the cobbler category: Seasonal fruits give the drink its freshness, ginger adds gentle spice, sake rounds it out, and the seaweed-infused tequila brings a contrast that really makes the drink pop.

1 handful seasonal fruits
1 oz / 3 cl sake
0.7 oz / 2 cl Don Julio Tequila, infused
with seaweed (see right)
0.3 oz / 1 cl ginger syrup (see page 221)

•

GARNISH
5–6 Pine needles
Absinthe

•

PREPARATION
Muddle the handful of fruits in the shaker, add the other ingredients, and shake hard over ice for about 10 seconds. Strain over crushed ice into the glass. Place the pine needles on the drink, spray with absinthe, then briefly sear the pine needles with a blowtorch.

•

Glass: highball glass

DON JULIO TEQUILA INFUSION WITH SEAWEED

Place 1 l tequila and 200 g seaweed in a large sealable container and infuse for 1 week, tasting every now and then—the infusion should have a hint of the sea. Then filter through a simple filter and pour into a clean bottle.

Cocktail No. 16

AROMA EXPLOSION

This drink is a twist on the famous classic Hot Buttered Rum. In my recipe, I use homemade date syrup and also add walnut flavors, which really bring out the taste of the Hennessy cognac. Butter makes the drink smooth, black pepper bitters add a nice subtle heat, and the cinnamon, orange peel, and cloves make it an absolute must on cold days.

1.7 oz / 5 cl Hennessy Fine de Cognac
0.3 oz / 1 cl date syrup (see page 221)
0.3 oz / 1 cl Lantenhammer Walnut Liqueur
1 oz / 3 cl still water
2 dashes Fee Brothers Walnut Bitters
3 dashes black pepper bitters
1 cinnamon stick
1 orange zest, studded with 2 cloves

•

TOPPING
4 tsp Unsalted butter

•

GARNISH
None

•

PREPARATION
Put everything in an ovenproof dish and heat it up, but don't let it boil. When the drink is hot enough, pour it into a champagne glass and top with the unsalted butter.

•

Glass: champagne glass

Cocktail No. 17

FIRE, HELP, FIRE

*My very personal twist on Jerry Thomas' famous Blue Blazer Cocktail
from 1862 .*

1.7 oz / 5 cl Booker's Bourbon Whiskey
0.3 oz / 1 cl Talisker Storm Whisky
0.3 oz / 1 cl Chartreuse VEP
2 dashes The Bitter Truth Grapefruit Bitters
2 bs stevia sugar

•

GARNISH
Grapefruit zest

•

PREPARATION
Put all the ingredients except the stevia sugar
into a heatproof metal grog glass and set
alight. Slowly pour it into a second heatproof
grog glass using the throwing method (see
page 231), lifting the stream high enough so
the flame is visible.

•

Glass: nosing glass

TIP

*Be extremely careful when pouring the
burning liquid. It's a good idea to practice
with water first until you get the hang of
throwing the cocktail.*

Cocktail No. 18

CIRCLE RAMOS SAKE FIZZ

I turned the famous classic Ramos Gin Fizz by Henry C. Ramos into a Japanese version with champagne. The original 1888 version of this cocktail was shaken for a full twelve minutes. Experts call this drink one of the best in the world, and ladies even say it tastes like a flower.

2 oz / 6 cl sake
1 oz / 3 cl fresh lemon juice
0.7 oz / 2 cl vanilla syrup (see page 222)
0.7 oz / 2 cl cream
1 egg white
5 dashes The Bitter Truth Orange Flower Water

•

TOPPING
8 cl Moët & Chandon Brut Champagne

•

GARNISH
Orange zest

•

PREPARATION
Shake vigorously in a shaker over ice for about 20 seconds and strain into a glass. Carefully top with champagne to give a nice foamy head. Garnish with orange zest.

•

Glass: highball glass

Cocktail No. 19

SEX ON THE BEACH

Sex on the Beach, a classic that almost all of us have ordered and drunk at least once, is but prepared here in a totally new way. Usually, I serve this drink inan edible condom-shaped gelatin envelope. But we're skipping that here, since that's really only for total pros.

1.7 oz / 5 cl Belvedere Vodka
1.4 oz / 4 cl best quality pomegranate juice
0.7 oz / 2 cl fresh lime juice
0.7 oz / 2 cl plum liqueur
0.3 oz / 1 cl demerara syrup (see page 221)
0.2 oz / 0.5 cl verjus
0.3 oz / 1 cl vanilla syrup (see page 222)

•

GARNISH
Dark chocolate
Almonds
Few drops of Lemon juice

•

PREPARATION
Make a chocolate-almond rim for the glass: Crush dark chocolate and blanched almonds together, rub the rim of the glass with a little lemon juice, and dip the glass into the chocolate-almond mix. Shake the ingredients for the drink in a shaker over ice for about 10 seconds and strain into the glass.

•

Glass: tumbler—Old Fashioned glass

Cocktail No. 20

FRENCH GIRL IN PARIS

This is a cocktail for the strong woman who wants a champagne cocktail with a real kick, lots of flavor, and notes of anise, honey, and vanilla. A tribute to the Air Mail Cocktail!

0.2 oz / 0.5 cl absinthe blanche
1.4 oz / 4 cl Bacardi 8 Rum
0.7 oz / 2 cl fresh lime juice
0.3 oz / 1 cl vanilla syrup (see page 222)

•

TOPPING
2.7 oz / 8 cl Moët & Chandon Brut Champagne

•

GARNISH
Maraschino cherry

•

PREPARATION

Rinse the champagne glass with absinthe, then pour out the excess. Shake all the other ingredients over ice in a shaker for about 10 seconds and strain into the glass. Top with champagne and garnish with a stemmed cherry.

•

Glass: champagne glass

Cocktail No. 21

SUPER MARGARITA

The Margarita, served with a salt rim in the classic glass, is surely familiar to everyone and has definitely given some of us a few fun nights. But here comes a slightly different version—smokier, fruitier in taste, with a slight sweetness and a subtly bitter finish.

1.7 oz / 5 cl Don Julio Blanco Tequila
0.3 oz / 1 cl Campari
0.7 oz / 2 cl fresh lime juice
0.7 oz / 2 cl fresh mandarin juice
0.3 oz / 1 cl dill syrup (see page 221)

•

GARNISH
Himalayan salt
Dill stalk

•

PREPARATION
Rim the glass with salt. Shake the ingredients in a shaker over ice for about 10 seconds and strain into the glass. Garnish with a sprig of dill.

•

Glass: tumbler—Old Fashioned glass

Cocktail No. 22

LIKE A ZOMBIE

Everyone's tried the Long Island Iced Tea at least once and thought it was the ultimate cocktail. But it's really not, and honestly, it's a shame about all the great spirits that get used for it. Based on those ingredients, we came up with a classy twist—a super smooth cocktail that's especially fun in the summer.

0.7 oz / 2 cl Tanqueray No. TEN Gin
0.7 oz / 2 cl Banks 5 Islands White Rum
0.7 oz / 2 cl Don Julio Blanco Tequila
0.7 oz / 2 cl Grand Marnier
0.7 oz / 2 cl ruby port
0.3 oz / 1 cl Fernet Branca
6.8 oz / 20 cl Coca-Cola

•

GARNISH
Lemon zest

•

PREPARATION
Build in a highball glass over ice and top up
with Coca-Cola. Garnish with a lemon twist.

•

Glass: tall highball glass

Cocktail No. 23

CIRCLE MILK PUNCH

Jerry Thomas' cocktail Milk Punch is the base for so many hot punches around the world. Our punch is also based on that recipe, with added flavor to make it delightfully bold as well as sweet. The sweetness of the drink should be something special too, so we went with rice-coconut milk, which is an awesome milk alternative.

1 oz / 3 cl Bacardi 8 Rum
1 oz / 3 cl Hennessy VS Cognac
2 oz / 6 cl rice-coconut milk
0.3 oz / 1 cl Demerara syrup (see page 221)

•

TOPPING
Chestnut espuma (see page 222)

•

GARNISH
Nutmeg
Star anise

•

PREPARATION
Shake vigorously in a shaker over ice for about 10 seconds, strain into a glass, and top with chestnut espuma. Grate nutmeg over the finished drink and garnish with star anise.

•

Glass: punch glass or toumbler—Old Fashioned glass

Cocktail No. 24

WINE VS. CHAMPAGNE

This punch is one of our bestsellers and it's actually my favorite in the summer. With wine, champagne, and a splash of cognac for that extra kick, it's a great drink that I love as an aperitif and/or after dinner when it's cooler.

1 oz / 3 cl Hennessy VS Cognac
1.7 oz / 5 cl dry Riesling white wine
0.3 oz / 1 cl still water
0.3 oz / 1 cl honey syrup (see page 221)

•

TOPPING
3.4 oz / 10 cl Moët & Chandon Brut Champagne

•

GARNISH
Dehydrated fruits
Fresh seasonal berries
Rosemary sprig

•

PREPARATION
**Build in the glass and top with champagne.
Stir well and garnish with fruits and a
rosemary sprig.**

•

*Glass: punch glass or
tumbler—Old Fashioned glass*

Cocktail No. 25

EGGNOG

This is a cocktail for tchilly days, with just the boost you need. It's in the eggnog category, which means it's made with raw eggs—no problem as long as you pay attention to freshness. Here too, regular milk is replaced by almond milk. Surprisingly, lots of young people order this cocktail—a sign that old-school drinks are getting more attention again.

1 oz / 3 cl Hennessy VS Cognac
1 oz / 3 cl Calvados
1 oz / 3 cl cream
1 oz / 3 cl almond milk
0.3 oz / 1 cl apple cider
2 dashes The Bitter Truth Jerry Thomas Bitters
1 egg

•

GARNISH
Dehydrated apple slices, caramelized with
brown sugar

•

PREPARATION
Shake well in a shaker over ice for about 10
seconds, then strain into a glass. Garnish with
apple slices.

•

*Glass: punch glass or
tumbler—Old Fashioned glass*

Cocktail No. 26

GRASSHOPPER 2.0

Don't freak out—yep, it's a real grasshopper, and yep, it's actually pretty tasty. With the right instructions, our "Grasshopper 2.0" is a real treat—plus, it looks awesome and was hands down the most talked-about and photographed cocktail at my bar "Circle." We took a closer look at the classic and thought about how we could turn it into a real grasshopper cocktail. Here's the result.

1.4 oz / 4 cl Tanqueray No. TEN Gin
0.5 oz / 1.5 cl Chartreuse VEP
0.3 oz / 1 cl fresh lemon juice
0.3 oz / 1 cl brown crème de cacao
0.3 oz / 1 cl sugar syrup (see page 222)
1 egg white
5 mint sprigs

•

GARNISH
Grasshopper
Mint sprig

•

PREPARATION
For the garnish, wash and pat dry the grasshopper, remove the wings, and dehydrate it. Shake all ingredients over ice in a shaker for about 10 seconds and strain into the glass. Garnish with plenty of mint and place the grasshopper on top of the mint.

•

Glass: tumbler—Old Fashioned glass

TIP

If you don't have a dehydrator, you can dehydrate the grasshopper in the oven too. Just dip the grasshopper in a little gin and brush with honey. Roast at 120°C /250°F (top/ bottom heat) for 20 minutes.

Cocktail No. 27

RUN, RUM, RUN

One of the best wake-up cocktails ever, this version of the Espresso Martini—is made with rum and rum liqueur. For this kind of cocktail, it's important not to use coffee from a machine, but to go for good quality coffee or espresso.

1.4 oz / 4 cl Bacardi 8 Rum
0.3 oz / 1 cl falernum
0.3 oz / 1 cl Grand Marnier
0.3 oz / 1 cl demerara syrup (see page 221)
0.7 oz / 2 cl espresso

•

GARNISH
Orange zest
Crushed coffee beans

•

PREPARATION
Shake well in a shaker over ice for about 10 seconds, then strain into a glass. Squeeze the orange zest over the drink and sprinkle it with the crushed coffee beans.

•

Glass: martini glass

Cocktail No. 28

WAKE ME UP BEFORE YOU GOGOOOOO

This wake-up cocktail is also based on an Espresso Martini. Similar to Cocktail No. 27, but here Bénédictine replaces the rum, and overall it has slightly more coffee flavor. Again, please use good quality coffee or espresso.

0.7 oz / 2 cl Bénédictine
0.3 oz / 1 cl Fernet Branca
2.4 oz / 7 cl espresso
3 dashes The Bitter Truth Grapefruit Bitters

•

GARNISH
Grapefruit zest

•

PREPARATION
Stir gently in a mixing glass over ice for
about 10 seconds and strain into the glass.
Garnish with grapefruit zest.

•

Glass: martini glass

Cocktail No. 29

THE FRENCH QUARTER

This is one of my personal favorites. I called it "The French Quarter" because it's inspired by the Vieux Carré Cocktail. The chestnut cream makes a super smooth cocktail that usually wins everyone's heart around midnight.

1 oz / 3 cl Michter's Rye Whiskey
1 oz / 3 cl Hennessy VS Cognac
1 oz / 3 cl red vermouth
3 dashes The Bitter Truth Aromatic Bitters
3 dashes Peychaud's Bitters or The Bitter
Truth Creole Bitters

•

TOPPING
Chestnut espuma (see page 222)

•

GARNISH
Crushed chestnuts

•

PREPARATION
Stir gently in a mixing glass for about 10 seconds and strain into a glass over ice. Top with chestnut espuma and garnish with chestnuts.

•

Glass: tumbler—Old Fashioned glass

Cocktail No. 30

AM I DRINKING A FLOWER

Summer, summer, summer ... the absolute favorite is floral, creamy, fruity. You just can't get enough of this drink, and thanks to the low alcohol content, it can be enjoyed any time of day. The verjus with grapes and honey is an awesome combo, rounded off perfectly by the botanicals in Cocchi Americano.

8 white seedless grapes
1.7 oz / 5 cl Cocchi Americano
0.7 oz / 2 cl verjus
0.5 oz / 1.5 cl honey syrup (see page 221)
1 egg white

•

TOPPING
4 cl soda water
6 dashes Peychaud's Bitters or
The Bitter Truth Creole Bitters

Kewra water spray

•

GARNISH
None

•

PREPARATION
Muddle the grapes in a shaker, add the other ingredients and shake hard over ice for about 10 seconds. Strain into a glass, top with soda water and bitters, and spritz with Kewra water.

•

Glass: tumbler—Old Fashioned glass

Cocktail No. 31

MEYHANE GECELERI

Raki, Pernod, pastis, absinthe, ouzo—anise drinks are dismissed as old-fashioned or just something to drink on vacation in southern countries. Totally unfair. Here we show you a raki cocktail you can enjoy with dinner in the evening or just sip straight. We're working on many more recipes with these awesome spirits and predict a trend coming up in the next few years.

3 cardamom pods
4 bs yogurt, caramelized with brown sugar
1 oz / 3 cl raki
3 dashes cardamom bitters
½ tsp ground cinnamon
0.7 oz / 2 cl honey syrup (see page 221)
0.3 oz / 1 cl espresso

•

GARNISH
Grated cinnamon

•

PREPARATION
Muddle cardamom pods in the shaker. Add yogurt and all the other ingredients and shake for about 10 seconds. Strain into a glass over ice and garnish with cinnamon.

•

Glass: cocktail coupe

Cocktail No. 32

HOW THEY CALL BANANA ...

How do you say a Banana Daiquiri in ... —who doesn't know that legendary scene from the movie "Scarface"? But somehow the banana flavor never really comes through, so we picked a banana eau de vie to bring that flavor into the drink—along with a bit of banana powder. Et voilà—the best Banana Daiquiri, you've ever tried.

1.4 oz / 4 cl Zacapa 23 Rum
0.7 oz / 2 cl Stählemühle Dessert Banana Eau de Vie
0.5 oz / 1.5 cl fresh lime juice
0.5 oz / 1.5 cl demerara syrup (see page 221)
½ tsp dried banana powder

•

GARNISH
Dehydrated banana slice

•

PREPARATION
Shake well in a shaker over ice for about 10
seconds, then strain into a glass. Garnish
with a banana slice.

•

Glass: cocktail coupe

Cocktail No. 33

ITALIAN SPRIZZ

Aperol Spritz has become the classic summer drink. But instead of wine or prosecco, we use the finest champagne and add a touch of lemon to turn it into a foam that, together with Aperol and aged balsamic, delivers an awesome flavor experience.

1.4 oz / 4 cl Aperol
6.8 oz / 20 cl champagne–lemon foam
(see right)

•

TOPPING
5 Drops aged balsamic

•

GARNISH
Dehydrated orange slice

•

PREPARATION
Pour Aperol into the glass and top up with champagne-lemon foam—the foam should be nice and firm. Then top with aged balsamic and garnish with orange.

•

Glass: champagne glass

CHAMPAGNE-LEMON FOAM
Put 300 ml (10.1 oz) champagne, 4 cl (1.4 oz) freshly squeezed lemon juice, and *2 egg whites* into an ISI cream whipper and shake briefly and vigorously. Aerate with 2 cream cartridges and chill.

Cocktail No. 34

STRAIGHT FROM THE FOREST

I still remember it so clearly: On one of the first beautiful sunny days of the year, I was out and about in Munich and heading towards the English Garden when I felt a spring breeze—and was inspired to create this cocktail. Fresh, easy to drink, elegant, and super smooth on the finish—the taste of spring. After a few tries, the recipe is now final and flawless.

2 oz / 6 cl Tanqueray No. TEN Gin, infused
with wild herbs and flowers (see right)

1 bs bee pollen syrup (see page 221)

2 dashes The Bitter Truth Lemon Bitters

•

TOPPING

Spray bergamot

•

GARNISH

None

•

PREPARATION

Stir in a mixing glass over ice for about 10 seconds and strain into a cocktail glass. Spray with bergamot spray.

•

Glass: cocktail coupe

TANQUERAY NO. 10 GIN INFUSION WITH WILD HERBS AND FLOWERS

Place 1 l (34 oz) Tanqueray No. TEN Gin , 75 g (2.6 oz) dandelion, 75 g (2.6 oz) sorrel, and *100 g (3.5 oz) daisies* into a sous-vide device and cook at 58 °C/136°F for about 2 hours. Chill, filter, and bottle.

Cocktail No. 35

THE FAMOUS GIN GIN PUNCH

This was our absolute "Circle" classic in the punch category, which has already made a name for itself as the Gin Gin Punch and is so quick to make. A super drinkable cocktail with flavors of vanilla, apple, and juniper that work any time of year—but it tastes best outside in the garden during summer.

1 oz / 3 cl Hendrick's Gin
1 oz / 3 cl Monkey 47 Gin
0.3 oz / 1 cl St. Germain elderflower liqueur
0.7 oz / 2 cl fresh lemon juice
0.7 oz / 2 cl vanilla syrup (see page 222)
1 oz / 3 cl Van Nahmen Boskoop apple juice

•

TOPPING
1.4 oz / 4 cl soda water, filtered with
Japanese Binchotan charcoal

•

GARNISH
Grated nutmeg
Dehydrated orange slice

•

PREPARATION
Shake vigorously in a shaker over ice for about 10 seconds, strain into a glass, and top with soda water. Grate nutmeg over the finished drink and pop the orange slice on top.

•

Glass: tumbler—Old Fashioned glass

Cocktail No. 36

NEW YORK, PARIS, MUNICH, TOKYO

You could totally call this drink "New York, Paris, Munich, Tokyo" because there's an ingredient from each country, and they all vibe perfectly together. A bit bolder in flavor, this is the kind of cocktail you enjoy with the guys in good company.

1 oz / 3 cl Michter's Rye Whiskey
1 oz / 3 cl Nikka from the Barrel Whisky
5 dashes The Bitter Truth Jerry Thomas Bitters

•

TOPPING
Spray of absinthe blanche

•

GARNISH
Sugar cube, flambéed with absinthe

•

PREPARATION
Stir in a mixing glass over ice for about 10 seconds, strain, and spray with absinthe. Then place the sugar cube on the drink, soak it with absinthe, and set alight.

•

Glass: tumbler—Old Fashioned glass

Cocktail No. 37

CARROT IN KENTUCKY

"The Carrot in Kentucky" ... is a cool name for the drink that's number 37 here. Whiskey, carrot, and eucalyptus are the main flavor players here, and together they make an awesome combo. A classic twist on the Old Fashioned Cocktail from the 19th century.

2 oz / 6 cl Michter's Rye Whiskey
0.3 oz / 1 cl carrot syrup (see page 222)
2 dashes The Bitter Truth Jerry Thomas Bitters
2 dashes eucalyptus bitters

•

TOPPING
Spray absinthe blanche

•

GARNISH
Lemon zest

•

PREPARATION
Stir in a mixing glass over ice for about 10 seconds, strain, and spray with absinthe. Garnish with lemon zest.

•

Glass: tumbler — Old Fashioned glass

Cocktail No. 38

ROASTED WITH SHERRY AND SWEETENED WITH HONEY

BBQ season is on, and we've got the perfect ultimate drink to go with it. Grilled pineapple flavors in the rum, plus grilled citrus and honey in the drink, give every dish just the right kick. A cold craft beer goes great with it, too.

2 oz / 6 cl Banks 7 Rum, infused with
grilled pineapple (see right)
1 oz / 3 cl fresh grilled lime juice
0.7 oz / 2 cl PX Sherry
0.2 oz / 0.5 cl honey syrup (see page 221)
2 dashes The Bitter Truth Orange Bitters

•

GARNISH
Dehydrated
Pineapple

•

PREPARATION
Shake vigorously in a shaker over ice for
about 10 seconds and strain. Garnish with
pineapple.

•

Glass: cocktail coupe

**BANKS 7 RUM INFUSION WITH
GRILLED PINEAPPLE**

*Chop up 1 pineapple into small pieces,
including the core. Grill the fruit on a charcoal
grill or in a dry ridged grill pan to create those
classic grill lines. Place into a sous-vide bag and
add the rum. Cook sous-vide at 60°C/140°F
for for 2 hours.*

GRILLED LIME JUICE
Cut the limes in half and cook in a grill pan
until the juice on the cut side caramelizes.
Cool slightly, then squeeze, pour into a clean
bottle bottle it up, and chill.

Cocktail No. 39

ADVANCED SMASH

A well-known classic gets a twist here with cucumber and rose water, with egg white for a cloud-like froth. The summer months will thank us for this one, because this drink goes down easily and is so refreshing too. Let's hope the hangover the next day isn't too bad ...

3 slices cucumber
1 handful basil
2 oz / 6 cl Rutte Celery Gin
1 oz / 3 cl fresh lime juice
0.7 oz / 2 cl ginger syrup (see page 221)
2 dashes The Bitter Truth Celery Bitters
2 dashes The Bitter Truth Rose Water
1 egg white

•

GARNISH
Basil leaf

•

PREPARATION
Muddle cucumber and basil in the shaker,
then shake hard with the other ingredients
and over ice for about 10 seconds. Double
strain the finished cocktail and garnish.

•

Glass: cocktail coupe

Cocktail No. 40

SEE IT LOOKS LIKE WATER

A glass of water that tastes just like a Whiskey Sour! The White Dog Whiskey, aged just a few days, is mixed with clarified lemon juice and sugar syrup—and voilà! It works great, it's a Whiskey Sour and tastes like one too, just without the color. Cheers.

2 oz / 6 cl white dog whiskey / legal moonshine
1 oz / 3 cl fresh lemon juice, clarified with
agar-agar (see right)
0.7 oz / 2 cl sugar syrup (see page 222)

•

GARNISH
Optional: Maraschino cherry

•

PREPARATION
Stir gently in a mixing glass over ice for about
30 seconds and strain. Optionally garnish with
a maraschino cherry.

•

Glass: tumbler—Old Fashioned glass

CLARIFIED LEMON JUICE
*In a pot, heat **200 ml (6.8 oz) freshly squeezed lemon juice** with **1.2 g (0.04 oz) agar-agar** to 95°C/203°F. Stir until the agar-agar is dissolved. Pour everything into a bag and freeze. After 24 hours, let the frozen block thaw slowly and strain it through a filter.*

SICHUAN PEPPER ESSENCE
Infuse 500 ml (17 oz) vodka with 2 handfuls of Sichuan pepper and 1 chili pepper for 48 hours. Strain.

Cocktail No. 41

TOMATO – CLAMATO

We've tweaked the famous Bloody Mary, one of the all-time classics, so that anyone can enjoy it. Here we use organic, high-quality tomato juice, mixed with strained tomatoes and a miso paste for that ultimate umami flavor.

1.7 oz / 5 cl Belvedere Vodka
5 oz / 15 cl tomato juice mix (see right)
0.3 oz / 1 cl fresh lemon juice
6 dashes Worcestershire sauce
2 dashes Sichuan pepper essence (see left)
0.04 oz / 1 g salt

•

GARNISH
⅛ Lemon

•

PREPARATION
Shake in a shaker over ice for just 3 seconds
and strain into a glass. Don't shake it any
longer, otherwise the cocktail will too diluted.
Garnish with lemon.

•

Glass: highball glass

TOMATO JUICE MIX
Dissolve 1 tsp miso paste in water, add 1 l (34 oz) organic tomato juice, 1 can of the best strained tomatoes, blend, then bottle.

Cocktail No. 42

JAPAN MEETS CHINA

Ultra-trendy for a few years now and still going strong. The Moscow Mule, originally invented by Smirnoff, is still on its winning streak. We "brew" our own ginger beer and spice up the drink with special ingredients to make it even more refreshing, spicier, and tastier.

1.7 oz / 5 cl Belvedere Vodka
5 oz / 15 cl homemade ginger beer (see right)
0.2 oz / 0.5 cl yuzu juice
2 dashes Sichuan pepper essence
(see page 146)

•

GARNISH
2 Slices cucumber

•

PREPARATION
Stir gently in a highball glass over ice.
Garnish with cucumber slices.

•

Glass: highball glass

HOMEMADE GINGER BEER
Mix 1 l (34 oz) freshly pressed ginger juice with 2 l (77 oz) fresh lemon juice, 3 l (101 oz) sugar syrup (see page 222), and 4 l (135 oz) water. Pour into a soda siphon and carbonate with a soda cartridge.

Cocktail No. 43

CHAMPAGNE FOR THE ADVOCAT

Avocado in a drink? With a frozen pit that replaces the ice cube? We'll to show you how it's done, and just a heads up: The next few summers will have a lot to do with this drink. Its mix of vermouth (with low alcohol content as a base), refreshing soda water, a splash of champagne, and bitters is just unbeatable.

2 oz / 6 cl Cocchi Americano, infused with
avocado (see right)
1.7 oz / 5 cl Moët & Chandon Brut Champagne
1.7 oz / 5 cl soda water
2 dashes Peychaud's Bitters

•

GARNISH
Ice-cold avocado pit, straight
from the freezer

•

PREPARATION
Put the avocado pit in the wine glass
and add the rest of the ingredients.Stir
gently.

•

Glass: wine glass

COCCHI AMERICANO INFUSION WITH AVOCADO

Cut open 2 avocados, remove the pits, scoop out the flesh with a spoon and chop. Put 1 l (34 oz) Cocchi Americano with the avocado flesh into a sous-vide bag and cook at 55°C /130°F for 2 hours. Strain, chill, and bottle.

Cocktail No. 44

WHITE TRUFFLE MARTINI

If you've got the cash, you can mix up this cocktail for yourself. I tried this drink for the first time in a luxury hotel—and I was brave enough to use white Alba truffle as an ingredient. If you love white truffle, you'll never get enough of this—it's super easy to make, and the taste is just amazing.

2 oz / 6 cl vodka, infused with white
Alba truffles (see right)
0.7 oz / 2 cl Noilly Prat Vermouth

•

GARNISH
1 Slice of white Alba truffle

•

PREPARATION
Stir in a mixing glass over ice for about 10
seconds. Garnish with truffle.

•

Glass: martini glass

VODKA INFUSION WITH WHITE ALBA TRUFFLES
Slice 1 g (0.04 oz) white Alba truffle. Put with 1 l (34 oz) vodka in a container and leave for at least 2 weeks, up to 4 weeks. The longer the truffle infuses, the stronger the flavor.

Cocktail No. 45

BERRY HONEY BERRY

Here comes the ultimate fruit cocktail, also known as a Cobbler. If you're craving lots of fruit and a little more sweetness than usual, this is your drink. You can mix up this drink with any fruits you like.

¼ mango, diced
¼ papaya, diced
3 strawberries, diced
3 raspberries
3 blackberries
2 oz / 6 cl Tanqueray No. TEN Gin
0.7 oz / 2 cl fresh lemon juice
0.7 oz / 2 cl honey syrup (see page 221)

•

GARNISH
Selection of fruits from the
ingredient list

•

PREPARATION
Gently muddle the fruits in a highball glass.
Then add all the other ingredients and gently
stir over ice. Garnish with your favorite fruits.

•

Glass: highball glass

Cocktail No. 46

ARIBAAAAA ...

Simple, pure, awesome! An excellent, easy-drinking cocktail you can enjoy anytime. Coriander, agave, lime, and tequila—mixed with smoked salt— just taste amazing together. This drink is always the highlight at any BBQ.

1.7 oz / 5 cl Don Julio Blanco Tequila
0.7 oz / 2 cl fresh lime juice
0.7 oz / 2 cl cilantro syrup (see page 222)
0.3 oz / 1 cl agave syrup

•

GARNISH
Smoked salt (see right)

•

PREPARATION
Shake well in a shaker over ice for about 10 seconds, then strain into a glass. Garnish with smoked salt.

•

Glass: tumbler—Old Fashioned glass

SMOKED SALT
Spread *sea salt on a tray and smoke it in a smoker for 1 hour.*

Cocktail No. 47

SIPPING AT THE BEACH

Cachaça became famous thanks to the Caipirinha, but more and more bartenders are using it for other cocktails too, and here it's making a real comeback. After long deliberation we went with this tropical version, which whisks our minds us to the beach, glass in hand.

5 small pieces grilled pineapple
(see page 140)
3 black peppercorns
1.7 oz / 5 cl Armazem Cachaça
0.7 oz / 2 cl fresh melon juice
0.7 oz / 2 cl rice milk

•

GARNISH
Pineapple leaves

•

PREPARATION
Muddle the grilled pineapple and black pepper
in a shaker. Add all the other ingredients,
shake hard over ice for about 10 seconds, and
strain into a glass. Garnish with pineapple
leaves.

•

Glass: highball glass

Cocktail No. 48

ITALIAN CHOCOLATE

We've got one last version of the Espresso Martini up our sleeve that we just have to share with you. Slightly sweeter in taste, but with chocolate and amaro, this cocktail is one of my favorite combos. If you love Espresso Martini, you definitely shouldn't skip this drink.

10 coffee beans
1.7 oz / 5 cl Bacardi 8 Rum
0.7 oz / 2 cl Amaro Nonino
1 double espresso
0.7 oz / 2 cl liquid dark bittersweet chocolate

•

GARNISH
Coffee beans
Powdered sugar

•

PREPARATION
Crush the coffee beans, shake them together
with the other ingredients in a shaker over
ice for 10 seconds, and strain into a glass.
Garnish with coffee beans and
powdered sugar.

•

Glass: cocktail coupe

Cocktail No. 49

VIVA LA MEXICO

Spicy, sweet, sour, fruity, and a bit bitter—that's how you'd describe this cocktail. It's a real all-rounder, perfect as a starter or an aperitif. As a snack on the side, serve small watermelon balls sprinkled with sea salt.

6 small pieces watermelon
½ jalapeño, diced
1.7 oz / 5 cl Mezcal Espadín
0.3 oz / 1 cl Chartreuse Verte
1 oz / 3 cl fresh lime juice
0.3 oz / 1 cl agave syrup
1 pinch sea salt

•

GARNISH
Edible flowers

•

PREPARATION
Crush the watermelon and jalapeño,
shake them with the other ingredients in a
shaker over ice for about 10 seconds, and
double strain into a glass. Garnish with
edible flowers.

•

Glass: tumbler—Old Fashioned glass

Cocktail No. 50

BIR TÜRK KAHVESI LÜTFEN

This drink is one of my classics. Back then, when I watched my first sip of Turkish coffee being made the traditional way, the idea for this was born. With ccognac—the perfect match—and vanilla, this is a dessert drink that leaves any conventional dessert far behind.

1.7 oz / 5 cl Hennessy Fine de Cognac
0.7 oz / 2 cl ruby port
0.3 oz / 1 cl vanilla syrup (see page 222)
1.4 oz / 4 cl brewed Turkish coffee

•

GARNISH
Crushed coffee beans

•

PREPARATION
Put everything in a shaker, add ice, and throw the drink (see page 231). Garnish with crushed coffee beans.

•

Glass: Turkish coffee pot

9 Creations from International Bartenders

For a few years now, I've been inviting different bartenders to Munich to show them our beautiful city, but also our bar and cocktail culture. That's how A lively exchange has developed, and real friendships have grown up. The recipes collected here are proof of unforgettable moments and mean even more to me because I'm also happy to visit some of these bartenders and show off Munich's bar skills as a guest in their cocktail bars.

**AGOSTINO
PERRONE**

Mulata
Daisy

↓

1.4 oz / 4 cl Bacardi Superior Rum
0.7 oz / 2 cl fresh lime juice
0.7 oz / 2 cl brown crème de cacao
1 bs fine sugar
½ bs fennel seeds
0.3 oz / 1 cl Galliano L'Autentico

•

GARNISH
Cocoa

•

PREPARATION
**Rim the glass with cocoa. EShake all the
ingredients except the Galliano L'Autentico in
a shaker over ice for about 10 seconds. First
pour the Galliano into the glass, then strain in
the contents of the shaker.**

•

Glass: cocktail coupe

CONNAUGHT BAR
*Agostino Perrone runs the famous
"Connaught Bar" in the hotel of the
same name in London. The bar manager,
who has Italian roots, is one of the
internationally best-known professional
bartenders and has already won hosts of
awards.*

GEOFFREY CANILLO

Banana Daiquiri

1 oz / 3 cl Smith & Cross Rum
0.3 oz / 1 cl crème de banane
0.3 oz / 1 cl orange curaçao
2 ½ bl cinnamon sugar
½ banana
40 g crushed ice

•

GARNISH
Grated cinnamon

•

PREPARATION
**Blend in the blender on the highest setting
for 20 seconds. Pour into a glass and sprinkle
with cinnamon.**

•

Glass: cocktail coupe

BALDERDASH
*Geoffrey Canillo's bar "Balderdash"
in Copenhagen is currently one of
the hottest spots in Europe. To make
his cocktails, he has developed some
really unusual techniques and practices
bartending at the absolute highest level.*

Gold Fashioned

BAR SHIRA AND DROR ALTEROVICH

0.5 oz / 1.5 cl Del Maguey Vida Mezcal
0.5 oz / 1.5 cl Highland Park 12 Whisky
1 oz / 3 cl Bols Genever
0.3 oz / 1 cl falernum
2 dashes Angostura Bitters
1 dash gold dust

•

GARNISH
Gold dust

•

PREPARATION
Stir all the ingredients in a mixing glass for about 10 seconds. Strain into a cocktail glass over a small ice block or ice cubes and garnish with gold dust.

•

Glass: cocktail coupe

IMPERIAL CRAFT COCKTAIL BAR
Partners, Bar Shira and Dror Alterovich, were the first to bring cocktail culture to Israel, and their hard work has been recognized with many nominations and awards. Their "Imperial Craft Cocktail Bar" is famous worldwide and regularly hosts guest bartenders from all over the globe, who step behind the bar for a night or two.

SERHAN KUSAKSIZOGLU

The Asian Experiment

1.7 oz / 5 cl Michter's Rye Whiskey
1 oz / 3 cl Cocchi Rosa Vermouth
3.4 oz / 10 cl plum liqueur
3 dashes The Bitter Truth Orange Bitters

•

GARNISH
Lemon zest

•

PREPARATION
Stir in a mixing glass over ice for about 10 seconds.
Strain into a glass and garnish with lemon zest.

•

Glass: cocktail coupe

LOBSTER BAR
Serhan Kusaksizoglu is now Global Director of "Bar and Concepts" for the Asian hotel group Shangri-La. Turkish-born Serhan started his career as head bartender at the famous "Schumann's" in Munich, and then went on to work at other top spots around the world. Shangri-La hotel bars are considered some of the best in the world—each one has its own unique design concept, all with Serhan Kusaksizoglu's personal touch.

**MAURO
MAHJOUB**

Negroni
Western

0.7 oz / 2 cl Wild Turkey Bourbon
0.7 oz / 2 cl Campari
0.7 oz / 2 cl Frangelico
0.7 oz / 2 cl Lillet Vermouth Rouge
1 dash The Bitter Truth Chocolate Bitters

•

GARNISH
Orange zest

•

PREPARATION
Stir in a mixing glass over ice for about 10 seconds.
Strain into a glass and garnish with orange zest.

•

Glass: tumbler—Old Fashioned glass

MAURO'S NEGRONICLUB
*Mauro Mahjoub, also known as "the
King of Negroni," made a real mark on
Munich's bar scene with his bar "Mauro's
Negroni Club." With over 4,000 bar
books collected at the Munich Campari
Academy—a lovely little bar museum—
he's the world's biggest cocktail book
collector and historian. His top-notch
bar has won numerous awards, and the
Negroni counter above the bar is the
absolute highlight.*

MARIAN
BEKE

Goldfinger Daiquiri

1.7 oz / 5 cl Brugal 1888
5 bs soursop juice, boiled with carrot pieces
1 bs pineapple and papaya chutney
0.7 oz / 2 cl fresh lime juice

•

GARNISH
Lemon zest
Barbeque spice
Charred lime leaf
Stalk of lemongrass

•

PREPARATION
Mix lemon zest and barbeque spice, then rim
the glass with a lemon-BBQ edge. Shake the
ingredients in the shaker for about 10 seconds,
nice and strong.

•

Glass: cocktail coupe

THE GIBSON

*Marian Beke's big break came at the
London bar "Nightjar." Countless videos
shot about him there and posted on
YouTube made him world-famous. Years
later, he finally made his dream come
true: he opened his own bar, "The Gibson,"
and immediately scooped up all the
international awards in the very first year.
He gives talks on his unique mixing style all
over the world.*

PANDAN SYRUP
Cut up 16 pandan leaves and blend them with 1 l (34 oz) sugar syrup in a blender. Add 6 drops of pandan extract and 2 g (0.07 oz) salt, and it infuse. Strain into a clean bottle.

NICO DE SOTO

L'Alligator, C'est Vert

1 oz / 3 cl Pernod Absinthe
1 oz / 3 cl coconut milk
1 oz / 3 cl pandan syrup (see left)
1 egg

•

GARNISH
Nutmeg

•

PREPARATION
Shake in a shaker without ice for 10 seconds. Fill a second shaker over ice, pour in the liquid, and shake for another 10 seconds. Strain into a glass and grate nutmeg over the finished drink.

•

Glass: flip glass

DANICO

Nico de Soto celebrated worldwide success with his first bar "Mace" in New York City. His second bar "Danico" in Paris, continues his signature style. His specialty is traveling the world and finding new flavors and spices to put into his cocktails. This constantly earns him recognition, and every year sees a new award or title.

PHILIPP BISCHOFF

Manhattan

1.5 oz / 4.5 cl Michter's Rye Whiskey
0.5 oz / 1.5 cl Mancino red vermouth
0.3 oz / 1 cl cherry brandy
2 dashes Angostura Bitters

•

GARNISH
Maraschino cherry

•

PREPARATION
Stir in a mixing glass over ice for about 10 seconds and strain into a glass. Garnish with a stemmed cherry.

•

Glass: cocktail coupe

MANHATTAN BAR AT THE REGENT HOTEL

After a long time at the Berlin hotel bar "Amano" Philipp Bischoff from Germany ended up all the way in Singapore. After bringing worldwide fame to the "Amano Bar," it was time for the born-and-bred Berliner to Asia and take on new challenges. Philipp nailed those challenges in his very first year and took "his" Manhattan Bar at the Regent Hotel to 11th place in the World's 50 Best Bars ranking, winning Asia's Best Bar.

TRIPLE SOUR MIX
Mix together 500 ml (17 oz) freshly squeezed lime juice, 500 ml (17 oz) freshly squeezed lemon juice, 350 ml (11.8 oz) freshly squeezed pink grapefruit juice, 250 ml (8.4 oz) freshly squeezed orange juice, 125 ml elderflower liqueur, and 200 g (7 oz) sugar and chill.

**ONURCAN AND
YIGITCAN GENCER**

Make Me Crazy

1.2 oz / 3.5 cl Altos Plata Tequila
0.3 oz / 1 cl Cointreau
0.3 oz / 1 cl Aperol
2 oz / 6 cl triple sour mix

•

GARNISH
Dried crushed black olives
Dried bread
Red pepper

•

PREPARATION
Shake in a shaker over ice for about 10
seconds, then strain into a glass. Garnish with
olives and bread, sprinkle with pepper.

•

Glass: tumbler—Old Fashioned glass

FINN KARAKÖY

*Turkish-born twin brothers Onurcan and
Yigitcan Gencer are currently shaking
up the cocktail scene between Europe
and Asia. The duo is particularly popular
n Turkey and its neighboring countries,
and is showered with awards. Their way of
taking bartending to a whole new level with
entertainment is unique and appreciated
by bartenders all over the world. The two
brothers also work as consultants and
introduce guests to cocktails in different
countries.*

Food & Cocktail Pairings

In your net of love I was caught like a fish / in your kitchen I stayed, suffering, a fish / now your love's knife opens my flesh red / and silently my blood runs on your love's table

All recipes are by Florian Gürster.

Grilled Shiitake Veggies

SEE PAGE 191

Steak Tartare
SEE PAGE 190
Cocktail No. 1
SEE PAGE 67

Steak Tartare

with sesame, pear, and chili

The classic steak tartare is served in bistros and restaurants all over the world. Florian adapted this recipe from his time at "Hakkasan" in London and added his own twist to it. So this classy classic is not only quick to make, but also perfectly matched to our cocktails and ready to serve for any evening party or a cozy lunch at home. We also love to eat this steak instead of sandwiches for afternoon tea.

INGREDIENTS

FOR 4 PEOPLE

1 ¼ pounds / 500 g beef tenderloin

1 ripe pear

1 fresh chili

1 fresh egg yolk

1 tbsp sugar

3 tbsp olive oil

1 tbsp light soy sauce

2 tbsp sweet chili sauce

Sea salt

Cracked black pepper

2 tbsp sesame oil

1.8 oz / 50 g white sesame seeds

PREPARATION

Cut the meat into thin strips. Finely chop with a sharp knife and put it in a bowl.

Grate the pear with the skin on; finely chop the chili. Use a fork to mix the pear and egg yolk into the meat and stir together. Carefully season with sugar, olive oil, soy sauce, chili sauce, chili, sea salt, pepper, and sesame oil.

Heat a pan without oil. Carefully toast the sesame seeds in it and crush them with a rolling pin. Stir into the meat mixture.

Heat the oil in the pan and quickly sear the meat on both sides in batches.

TIP

We like to shape the steak tartare in a metal or plastic ring, which we remove before serving. Freshly toasted rustic rye bread goes well with it.

GRILLED SHIITAKE

Preheat the grill to 180 degrees and lightly oil the grill rack. **Wipe the mushroom caps** with a damp paper towel. **Mix lemon juice, salt, pepper,** and **garlic** with plenty of **olive oil** and brush the mushroom gills with it. Grill with the gill side up for 5–8 minutes.

Cocktail No. 1

A classic American root beer or a cold lager go fine with fillet of beef. But our Cocktail No. 1 (see page 67) is the ideal match. The whiskey infusion with Kobe beef fat goes perfectly with the flavors of the steak tartare.

Cocktail No. 5
SEE PAGE 75

Balsamic
Zucchini
SEE PAGE 195

Prawn Toast
SEE PAGE 194
↓

Prawn Toast

with Amai Sauce

For years now, the famous prawn toasts have been ordered as a snack or with a starter platter, and they're now a house classic. The big plus: This recipe can be prepped ahead of time, and it's perfect for any party where seafood is the star—even on hot days or down on the beach.

INGREDIENTS

FOR 4 PEOPLE

1 lime

2.2 lb / 1 kg raw shrimp

1.1 oz / 30 g garlic

3.5 oz / 100 g fresh ginger

1 bunch cilantro root

1 fresh chili

Sea salt

2 tbsp olive oil

1.8 oz / 50 g Sriracha sauce

4 slices toast

1.8 oz / 50 g butter

Oil for the tray

PREPARATION

Zest the lime. Finely chop the shrimp, garlic, ginger, and cilantro roots, and mix well. Season with chili, sea salt, lime zest, olive oil, and Sriracha sauce, to taste.

AMAI SAUCE

is a mix of tomato sauce, lemongrass, tom yum paste, honey, and soy sauce, available from Asian stores.

> **TIP**
>
> *To checkthe seasoning of the shrimp mixture, fry a llittle in a pan with some butter, and test it.*

Preheat the oven to 150°C /300°F top/ bottom heat and brush a baking tray with oil. Spread the shrimp mixture onto the slices of toast. Heat a little butter in a pan. Put the toasts in, toast the bottom, then flip and fry the shrimp side for 2 minutes each. Place them on the baking tray and bake in the oven for 5 minutes. Serve right away with the Amai sauce on the side.

BALSAMIC ZUCCHINI

Preheat the grill to medium-low heat and lightly oil the rack. **Slice the zucchini** 2 mm thick and brush them with **olive oil**. Season with **garlic powder, Italian seasoning** and **salt**. Grill on the preheated grill for 3–4 minutes on each side, until browned. Brush with **balsamic vinegar** and grill for 1 more minute. Serve right away.

Cocktail No. 5

Cocktail No. 5 (see page 75) is a superb pairing for the prawn toasts. The flavors of maple syrup and pumpkin-infused Michter's whiskey go well with chili and Sriracha sauce.

Cocktail No. 15
SEE PAGE 95
Pimientos de Padrón
SEE PAGE 199
Vintage Sardines
SEE PAGE 198

Vintage Sardines

from the can (Cihan's favorite)

We know the regular canned sardines from the supermarket. But they only become ultimate vintage sardines with this recipe, which gives that final kick with a hint of citrus and the mild heat of spring onions. I originally found this perfect bar snack in Japanese bar books and immediately fell in love with it. The fact that it's turned out to be the best companion for drinks and cocktails is probably thanks to the team of lots of olive oil and rye bread, which both help slow down the effects of alcohol in the blood. I often serve the sardines at Asia-style parties and at male-heavy event.

INGREDIENTS

FOR 4 PEOPLE

4 cans vintage Breton sardines in olive oil

½–2 lemons

4 spring onions

8 slices sourdough rye bread

PREPARATION

Pop open the can and place it on a plate, leaving the sardines inside the can. Squeeze half a lemon or more (to taste) and drizzle it over the sardines. Chop the spring onions finely and sprinkle them over the sardines.

TIP

Take the sardines out of the can one by one and enjoy. If you want, dip the bread in the sauce or just eat it on the side.

PIMIENTOS DE PADRON

In a big pan, heat up plenty of **olive oil** until hot. **Add Spanish pimientos** and fry, stirring. As soon as the first pimientos start to blister, take the pan off the heat. Sprinkle with top-quality English **Maldon salt flakes** and serve very hot.

Cocktail No. 15

A good white wine like a Chablis or Riesling goes perfectly with the sardines, of course, but we also have the ideal drink for this: Cocktail No. 15 (see page 95), which mixes fresh fruit with the kick of ginger and the flavors of sake and seaweed. One drink per can of sardines should be enough.

Cocktail No. 22
SEE PAGE 108
Baby Back Ribs
SEE PAGE 202
Sesame Snow
Peas
SEE PAGE 203

Baby Back Ribs

with Asian crust

These baby back ribs are the highlight of every party. I personally serve them at every Super Bowl or NBA Finals, when friends and buddies gather at my place and we spend the nights with ribs, beer, and cocktails while watching our favorite American sports. But they wouldn't be our ribs if we didn't have our own special recipe for them. The pure flavor experience comes from the Asian spice crust, which brings a whole range of flavors.

INGREDIENTS

FOR 4 PEOPLE

4.4 lb / 2 kg mini spareribs
3.5 oz / 100 g fresh ginger
1 clove fresh garlic
1 chili
2 stalks lemongrass
Oil for the sheet pan

MARINADE

3.5 oz / 100 g ketchup
1.1 oz / 30 g honey
1 jar hoisin sauce

GARNISH

Asian-spiced mixed nuts
7 oz / 200 g spring onions
1 chili, sliced into rings (optional)

PREPARATION

Fill a pot with cold water. Add the spareribs with all the other ingredients and simmer on low heat for about 1 hour to give a flavorful stock. Take out the spareribs, let them cool, and rest in the fridge for 1 hour. Preheat the oven to 180°C /350°F top/bottom heat. Oil a sheet pan. For the marinade, mix together ketchup, honey, and hoisin sauce. Generously marinate the spareribs and place them on the sheet pan. Pop them in the oven and cook for about 10 minutes until done. Meanwhile, chop the nuts and finely slice the spring onions. Sprinkle over the finished spareribs.

SESAME SNOW PEAS

Heat **sesame oil** in a large pan until almost smoking, then lower the heat slightly.. **Add the peas** and fry for about 1 minute, stirring occasionally. Take off the heat and season with **lemon juice**. Set aside, cover partially with a plate, and let rest briefly. After 5 minutes, check if the peas are as crunchy but tender as you want. Season with **salt** and **pepper**.

Cocktail No. 22

The perfect match for our baby back ribs is definitely Cocktail No. 22 (see page 108), a twist on *Long Island Iced Tea*, which is so easy to make. It shines with notes of port wine and Fernet Branca, but also the refreshing zing of Coca-Cola. It's not about lots of alcohol here, but all those awesome flavors.

Cocktail No. 29
SEE PAGE 123
Poached Egg
SEE PAGE 206
Steamed Broccoli
SEE PAGE 207

Poached Egg

with Truffle and Fried Potatoes

Sounds simple, Well, it is—but this dish is anything but a basic country meal, even if eggs and potatoes are the main ingredients. That's mostly thanks to the truffles, which turn this treat into a real feast for the taste buds. Poaching eggs—in my opinion, the best way to cook them—might take a little practice, but if you love poached eggs, you'll happily accept a few failed attempts.

INGREDIENTS

FOR 4 PEOPLE

EGGS

68 oz / 2 l water

3 tbsp white wine vinegar

4 eggs

½ Perigord truffle

POTATOES

1.8 lb / 800 g waxy potatoes

3.5 oz / 100 g butter

2 tbsp olive oil

QUARK

14 oz / 400 g quark (soft cream cheese)

Olive oil

Salt

Pepper

Chives

PREPARATION

Bring the water to a simmer and add the vinegar. Have two spoons ready. Carefully slide the eggs into the pot. Now gently push the egg white over the yolk with two spoons, so the white doesn't fray apart. Use the spoons to gently fold the egg white over the yolk and prevent it from "fraying." Poach the eggs for 3 minutes until the whites are set. Take them out and briefly refresh in salted water.

Serve the eggs on a plate and shave truffle over them.

Boil the potatoes in a large pot of water them until done. Let them steam off for a bit, peel, and roughly chop. Heat plenty of butter and olive oil in a cast iron pan and fry the potatoes until crispy. Mix the quark with all the other ingredients, season to taste, and serve with the potatoes.

STEAMED BROCCOLI

Peel the garlic cloves and slice thinly. Heat **olive oil** in a small pot over medium heat and sauté the garlic until light brown. **Add soy sauce** and **honey**, then simmer gently for 1 minute. **Squeeze the lime.** Add 1 tbsp **lime juice** and **sesame oil** to the soy mixture and set aside.

Toast the sesame in a dry pan until light brown. **Wash the broccoli** and break it into small florets. Peel the stalk with a vegetable peeler, slice it thinly, and line the bottom of a steamer basket with the slices. Place the broccoli florets on top.

Place a few inches of water in a pot with a tight-fitting lid and put the steamer basket inside. Bring to a boil, and steam the broccoli for 6–7 minutes. Take the broccoli out of the steamer and toss it with the sauce. Sprinkle with **sesame** and serve.

Cocktail No. 29

We'd suggest wine, beer, champagne, and Cocktail No. 29 (see page 123) as drinks to go with this dish. Whiskey and cognac for their spice, and chestnut espuma because it brings everything together and adds another layer of flavor. I'd serve the dish and cocktail in an more exclusive setting.

SEE PAGE 124

Pumpkin with
Balsamic and
Parmesan
SEE PAGE 210

Croque Monsieur
SEE PAGE 210

Croque Monsieur

with truffled Brie

Croque Monsieur first made an appearance in a Parisian café back in 1910. For me, it's one of the most classic bar snacks ever and every bistro, café, and bar should have it on the menu because it's got everything a bar snack needs: With just a few ingredients—brioche or white bread, cheese, ham, and lots of butter—it's so easy to make and promises maximum enjoyment, as long as you do it right, at "Brasserie Kämp" in Helsinki, where they serve amazing Croque Monsieur.

INGREDIENTS

FOR 4 PEOPLE

8 slices toast or brioche

3.5 oz / 100 g butter

2 tbsp oil

4 slices cooked ham

10.6 oz / 300 g truffled Brie (from the deli)

PREPARATION

Lightly spread butter on 4 slices of toast.
Top each with a slice of ham and cheese.
Place the remaining toast slices on top.

Heat butter and oil in a pan. Fry the toast
sandwich on both sides until golden brown.
Cut into triangles and serve.

PUMPKIN WITH BALSAMIC AND PARMESAN

Heat **oil** in a cast iron pan to medium. Once
the oil is hot, add **thyme** and **sage**. Slice a
pumpkin into strips, add to the pan, and
coat with oil. Fry for 5 minutes, stirring
occasionally. Turn down the heat and fry
the pumpkin for another 10 minutes until it's
roasted on all sides. Even if some pieces look

a little too roasted, just keep stirring until the middle is soft. Meanwhile, quickly mix together **balsamic vinegar** and **olive oil** and set aside.

Once the pumpkin is very tender, sprinkle with **salt** and **pepper**. Spread it out on a plate and add the balsamic vinaigrette. **Shave some Parmesan** over big flakes and serve right away.

Cocktail No. 30

When we were looking for the perfect match for Croque Monsieur, Cocktail No. 30 (see page 124) instantly came to mind—it ticks all the boxes. With its fruity notes, it's very refreshing, and the lower alcohol makes it the perfect drink any time of day: at lunchtime with a snack, or as a start to the evening when the sandwich isserved in bite-size pieces.

Crispy Salt and Vinegar
Potatoes

SEE PAGE 215
↓

Homemade Blue
Cheese Croissant
SEE PAGE 214

Cocktail No. 24
SEE PAGE 112

Homemade Blue Cheese Croissant

Croissant for breakfast? Classic. Croissant with blue cheese? Sensational. Croissant with blue cheese and kimchi? The ultimate making the leap from France to Asia—super easy to make and a real treat from the very first bite. Once you cut it in half, it's perfect for a late-night hunger pangs.

INGREDIENTS

FOR 4 PEOPLE

7 oz / 200 g blue cheese (room temperature)
8.8 oz / 250 g butter (room temperature)
1 package puff pastry
7 oz / 200 g flour
7 oz / 200 g kimchi (from Asian stores)
3 egg yolks
1 pinch sea salt
1 pinch cracked black pepper

PREPARATION

Mix the cheese and butter together until light and fluffy. Roll out the puff pastry, sprinkle with enough flour, and cut into triangles (any size you like). Spread to the edges with the cheese mixture.

Preheat the oven to 180°C top/bottom heat. Line a sheet pan with parchment paper.

Chop the kimchi into small pieces. Put 1 tablespoon of kimchi on each triangle, then roll them up into croissants. Brush with egg yolk and bake in the oven for about 15 minutes until golden. Sprinkle with salt and pepper.

CRISPY SALT AND VINEGAR POTATOES

Cut Potatoes cut in half, put in a pot, and cover with water about two fingers deep. **Add salt** and **vinegar** and bring to a boil. After 25–30 minutes, drain the potatoes.

Preheat the oven to 220°C and line a baking sheet with parchment paper. Toss the potatoes generously with **olive oil** and spread them out on the pan. Bake in the oven for 35 minutes, stirring every 5 minutes to make sure the potatoes don't burn. Once crispy, take them out of the oven. Season with **salt** and sprinkle with **chives**.

Cocktail No. 24

What goes with a croissant and blue cheese? That's a tricky one—but we came up with a drink that's perfect for the France–Asia combo: Cocktail No. 24 (see page 112) with cognac, white wine, a hint of honey, and a champagne topping. The fruit served in the drink adds just the right freshness.

Sweet Potato
Fries

SEE PAGE 219
↓

Cocktail No. 18
SEE PAGE 100

Club Sandwich
SEE PAGE 218

Club Sandwich

with chicken and mango mayo

The famous club sandwich can be found in every luxury hotel around the world and in countless variations—ranging from delicious to so-so. Our head chef has tweaked the original version to suit our guests' taste and created a subtly Asian-inspired variation. It fits any occasion, of course, because the bite-sized pieces are easy to serve and just as quick to eat. Winner, winner, chicken dinner!

INGREDIENTS

FOR 4 PEOPLE

1 tomato

1 baby romaine lettuce

1 jar mayonnaise

1 mango

1 jar chili pickles (from the Asian stores)

4 tbsp ketchup

Mustard

Some butter

4 eggs

8 slices bacon

2 fresh chicken breasts

12 slices toast

PREPARATION

Cut the tomatoes and lettuce into strips. Mix mayonnaise with mango and pickles, ketchup, and mustard into a tasty, spicy dip. Fold it into the lettuce.

Heat a pan with butter. Fry the eggs, bacon, and chicken breasts one after the other and set each aside. Slice the chicken breasts in half horizontally.

Toast the toast. For each serving, layer 3 slices of toast alternately with lettuce, egg, chicken, bacon, and tomato. Finally, secure it all with a wooden skewer.

SWEET POTATO FRIES

The day before, cut the **potatoes** into fries. Soak them in water so the starch washes out overnight.

Drain the fries, dry them, and briefly fry them at a low temperature in **peanut oil**. Cool slightly, return to the hot peanut oil, and finish frying. **Salt, pepper** and—if you like—**chili salt**.

Cocktail No. 18

The *Ramos Gin Fizz* is a cocktail that, in its original version, is shaken for 12 minutes. If you've got the muscle, you can do it quicker—or just try our version, Cocktail No. 18 (see page 100), which is based on sake and tastes super fresh thanks to the champagne. That's how the British club sandwich gets an Asian twist—an awesome combo, if you ask us. Enjoy!

Juices, Syrups, and Espumas

Without ingredients like juices, syrups, espumas (foams), some cocktail categories just don't work. Only the best and freshest juices should be used here. That's why we skip store-bought citrus juices. Squeeze fresh fruit to order or at least prep it the same day to get the perfect balance of acidity and sweetness that's needed for sours or fizzes. And when it comes to sweetness or toppings, there are lots of ways to create flavors, here are a few ideas.

SYRUPS

BEE POLLEN SYRUP

Mix **200 g (7 oz) bee pollen** with **300 g (10.6 oz) white sugar**. Add to **1 l (34 oz) water** and bring to a quick boil. Cool. Strain, pour into a clean bottle, and chill. Shelf life: 1 week.

DATE SYRUP

Pit and halve **500 g (17.6 oz) dates**. Bring **500 ml (17 oz) red port wine** and **500 ml (17 oz) sugar syrup** (see page 222) to a boil, reduce the heat by half, and let it simmer. Then stir in **100 ml (3.4 oz) cognac**. Let the syrup simmer on low heat until the volume is reduced by half. Cool. Roughly strain, pour into a clean bottle and chill.

DEMERARA SYRUP

Bring **500 g (17.6 oz) brown sugar** and **1 l (34 oz) hot water** to a boil. Once the sugar has dissolved, let it cool and pour into a clean clear bottle. Shelf life: 2 weeks.

DILL SYRUP

Bring **1 l (34 oz) sugar syrup** (see page 222) to a boil. Then prepare a pot of boiling water and another with cold water. **Quickly dip 1 bunch of dill** from the market into a pot of hot water, take it out right away and chill it in cold water over ice for at least 1 minute. Now add the dill to the boiled sugar syrup and let it simmer on medium heat for 5 minutes. Turn the heat all the way down and let it steep for 1 hour. Cool down. Strain into a clean bottle and chill.

HONEY SYRUP

Gently heat **500 g (17.6 oz) good (forest) honey** with **500 ml (17 oz) water** over low heat. Keep stirring until the honey has dissolved.
Honey syrup with wheat and bitters: **Mix 250 g (8.8 oz) honey** (preferably a rich forest honey) with **100 ml (3.4 oz) boiling hot water** until the honey thins and runs off the spoon. Then add **a handful of wheat grains** and **8 drops of whiskey barrel aged bitters** and boil on high heat for 2–3 minutes. To remove the wheat grains, strain through a medium sieve. Cool and use as needed. Shelf life: 3–4 days.

> *Honey syrup is awesome as a sweetener and I use it all the time. It gives cocktails a special touch and goes great with both dark and light spirits.*

GINGER SYRUP

Slice **100 g (3.5 oz) ginger**. Bring **1 l (34 oz) sugar syrup** (see page 222) to a boil and let it simmer on medium heat. Add the ginger slices, remove from heat and let it steep for 1 hour. Cool, strain into a clean bottle and chill.

CARROT SYRUP

Peel and chop 1 kg (2.2 lb) carrots. Bring to a boil in **1 l (34 oz) sugar syrup** (see below), reduce the heat by half and let it simmer. Then add **100 ml (3.4 oz) carrot juice** and stir. Let the syrup simmer on low heat until the volume is reduced by half. Cool, strain, pour into a clean bottle and chill.

CORIANDER SYRUP

Bring 1 l (34 oz) sugar syrup (see below) to a boil. Then prepare a pot of boiling water and another of iced water. **Quickly dip 1 bunch of market-fresh cilantro** into boiling water, remove immediately, and plunge into the iced water for at least 1 minute. Now add the cilantro to the sugar syrup and let it simmer over medium heat. Turn the heat all the way down and let it steep for 1 hour. Cool, strain into a clean bottle, and chill.

MATCHA SYRUP

Bring 1 l (34 oz) sugar syrup to a quick boil with **2 tsp matcha tea powder** while stirring constantly. Take it off the heat and let it infuse for 2–3 hours. Strain through a fine filter and chill.

> These days, the market is flooded with all kinds of bar syrups, and it's tough to find the right one for you and your needs. That's why we make our own syrups and show you here, step by step, how it's done.

TOGARASHI SYRUP

Mix 15 g (0.5 oz) togarashi with **1 l (34 oz) sugar syrup** (see below) and bring to a boil. Let it infuse in a cool place for 1 hour. Strain through a coffee filter and pour into a clean bottle.

VANILLA SYRUP

Scrape out 2 vanilla pods; set aside the pods and the seeds. **Bring 1 l (34 oz) sugar syrup** (see below) to a boil, add the vanilla pods and seeds, and stir constantly. Take it off the heat and let it infuse for 1 hour. Strain, pour into a clean bottle and chill.

> Togarashi is also known as shichimi spice, and is made from seven different ingredients: mandarin peel, red chili peppers, sesame seeds, poppy seeds, hemp seeds, nori, and ground sansho, a relative of Sichuan pepper.

CIGAR SYRUP

Crush 1 whole cigar and put it into **1 l (34 oz) hot sugar syrup** (see below). Here's the trick: Let it infuse for 15–20 seconds, no longer, otherwise the syrup gets too aromatic and will irritate the throat later. Strain immediately and chill. Then pour into a clean bottle.

SUGAR SYRUP

Bring 500 g (17.6 oz) white sugar to a boil with **1 l (34 oz) hot water**. Once the sugar has dissolved, let it cool and pour into a clean clear bottle. Shelf life: 2 weeks.

ESPUMAS

CHESTNUT ESPUMA

Fill 150 g (5.3 oz) ready-made chestnut cream into a cream siphon. **Mix in 2 egg whites, 2 cl (0.7 oz) sugar syrup** (see below), and **350 ml (12 oz) whole milk**. Stir well with a long spoon and put the lid on. Aerate with 2 cream cartridges and shake vigorously for 1 minute. Chill for 2 hours.

COCONUT ESPUMA

Mix 350 ml (12 oz) coconut milk with **100 ml (3.4 oz) whole milk** . **Mix in 5 cl (1.7 oz) sugar syrup** and **2 egg whites** and combine well. Fill into a cream siphon. Shake it well and aerate with 2 cream cartridges. Shake for another minute and chill.

> *"Being creative is easy, but actually coming up with an idea is the hard part."*
>
> *Ferran Adrià*

THE 6 MOST IMPORTANT JUICES AT THE BAR

APPLE JUICE

When it comes to apple juice, you can decide which type of juice you want to use for which drink. Of course, I'd always prefer fresh apple juice here too, but for many classic cocktail recipes, a good quality bottled cloudy apple juice is totally fine for everyday use. We personally use a mix of fresh and cloudy apple juice from the Boskoop region, which stands out for its fine acidity and adds a really nice touch to the cocktail's flavor.

LIME JUICE

Limes—made famous by the cocktails *Mojito* and *Caipirinha*—are now available in every well-stocked supermarket. Prices can vary depending on the season. The bar rules here: Always use fresh lime juice, never put whole limes in the glass, and only use the juice.

ORANGE JUICE

I personally treat myself to a glass of freshly squeezed orange juice every day. If I can find them, a blood orange from Sicily is the absolute best for me, but of course a regular orange does the trick too. I have the same standards for my drinks: They'd only suffer if I used a store-bought product or, even worse, a concentrate. A tequila or vodka with fresh blood orange juice and a dash of bitters can totally be the highlight of any summer.

PINK GRAPEFRUIT JUICE

Still in its infancy just a few years ago, pink grapefruit has now made its way into top bars and is increasingly popping up in bartenders' new cocktail creations. Same goes here: Please don't use store-bought juices—fresh fruit is even better because the peel is sturdy and can be easily removed and used as a garnish. After every squeeze, you should quickly check the acidity of the pink grapefruit so you can adjust the cocktail amounts accordingly.

> *"The freshness of the ingredients is the most important thing for syrups and juices, because it shows in the taste and also makes them last longer."*

TOMATO JUICE

This is the first time you're actually allowed to use a store-bought product. But please, only go for the highest quality you can get. Try out lots of juices before you pick the absolute best one—whether it's for home, private use, your bar, or your restaurant. In many cases, the juice will be used for the *Bloody Mary* cocktail. We actually use a mix of green and unripe red tomatoes and "clarify" them—so we basically serve a "clarified" *Bloody Mary*, that's as clear as a glass of water.

LEMON JUICE

Lemon juice is used as an acidifier for food and drinks, and is even said to have healing properties. Since it's in so many classic cocktails, it plays a key role at the bar too. Lemon juice should always be fresh, ideally squeezed right before you use it—seriously, stay away from pre-made stuff. Bars that don't have time to squeeze lemons fresh for every order can of course juice them ahead of time. Before bottling the fresh juice, you should definitely taste it, since the acidity can vary a lot and you want the perfect acidity for the perfect cocktail. Shelf life: up to 3 days in the fridge.

Equipment

Bar tools are the be-all and end-all of every bar. A good chef with a dull knife is like a bartender with a bad shaker. So it's a good idea to check out what tools are available and get the best equipment for the kind of cocktails you like to make. Most high-quality products come from Japan, the USA, and the UK. But Russia has also stepped up lately and their products are getting a lot of positive feedback from bartenders.

In our bar, we only use tools from Japan and the USA. So we use knives with the typical Japanese single-sided edge and sharpen them almost every day. We recommend getting sturdy tools, even if you have to spend a little more at first. The cheaper options end up costing more in the long run since you have to replace them more often.

The bartender's tools

1 BAR SPOON

Various companies like Cocktail Kingdom have shaken up the market with superb products and launched new designs. At the bar, you should have different sizes ready and try out which one works best for you.

"Japanese bar tools are our favorite when we get new equipment. The price might seem high, but the quality and durability speak for themselves."

2 SHAKER

The deciding factor for which shaker to use is what kind of cocktails you're making. For recipes with lots of juice, like Tiki drinks, we recommend the Boston shaker. It has a glass part and a metal part, and it's great because it holds a lot. The good thing about more space is that you can mix ingredients that are usually hard to combine.

The Japanese three-piece Cobbler shaker, on the other hand, is easy to use and often used at home. But pros use it too for the Japanese "hard shake," which takes years of practice to master. The two-piece metal shaker, also called the Tin Tin shaker, is perfect for short drinks with just a few ingredients, like *Daiquiri* or *Whiskey Sour.* Here, you shake fast and hard to get the result you want as quickly as possible. For a better grip and to shake more efficiently, we recommend holding the shaker horizontally.

3 MIXING GLASS

When it comes to mixing glasses, a Japanese mixing glass is the best option. A pro bartender should get two different sizes for making one or several cocktails at a time. Again, go for the best quality and make sure the mixing glass has no cracks or chips before you buy it. To keep the mixing glasses at the perfect temperature, we store them in the freezer until we need them.

4 MEASURING CUP (JIGGER)

Measuring cups come in all sorts of sizes, from 0.5 to 10 cl. The standard jigger is made up of two parts, one larger and one smaller. We love using measuring cups from Cocktail Kingdom in dual sizes like 3 cl and 6 cl or 2 cl and 5 cl, which come in different colors. But way more important than looks is how sturdy it is and that the jigger feels good to hold.

5 BAR STRAINER

We also look for quality in shaker strainers and prefer Hawthorne strainers. Wüsthof is the market leader here. The double strainer can be a regular one. The Hawthorne strainer can fit any shaker thanks to its spring edge, which should be flexible.

6 BAR KNIFE (BARKNIFE)

Japanese knives are a real advantage here, even if they need a lot of care. But if you take care of them, they'll last a long time, and replacement blades are available at any well-stocked specialty store. It's very important to learn the right cutting and sharpening techniques. Get some advice on which knife is best for you. You can try out sample cuts almost everywhere, so take advantage of that. Good knife work is just as important as having a good shaker at the bar.

With this basic equipment, you can mix all kinds of drinks at home:

1. Bar spoon, 2. Cobbler shaker, 3. Mixing glass, 4. Measuring cup (jigger), 5. Bar strainer, 6. Bar knife (barknife), 7. Citrus press

---

The quality of the tools and spirits you buy are some of the most important aspects for your home bar. Less is more, and you definitely need pro-level gear for your setup.

---

7 CITRUS PRESS

If you use the press a lot, every extra cent you spend on it is worth it in the long run. A nice bonus is that, if you use it right, your cocktail is enhanced not only by the juice, but also the essential oils. Presses come in different sizes; we use ones that work for both lemons and limes. We squeeze oranges and grapefruits by hand or use a citrus machine.

8 ICE SAW

Hard to find in Germany—this one's imported from Japan. The ice saw has a special shape, feels great in your hand, and is razor-sharp. It takes a few months to learn the right technique and prep the ice block properly.

9 SWIZZLE STICK

Used to stir up rum cocktails. Hold the stick between both palms, move one hand forward and the other in the opposite direction, so the cocktail mixes with the crushed ice.

10 ZESTER

Long and short zests, mostly from citrus fruits, your cocktail is enhanced not only by the juice, but also the essential oils. the aroma of cocktails. There are all kinds of zesters in different shapes and price ranges—figure out which one works best for you.

11 BAR TONGS

The reason bartenders use bar tongs is simple: Fruits, ice cubes, or other ingredients shouldn't be touched by hand. Simple tongs are fine for this, but if you want something special, hunt for vintage ones at flea markets—or travel to Argentina, where you'll find the coolest ones.

12 DOUBLE STRAINER

A fine strainer used after the drink has already been strained through a regular strainer. This second step is necessary to catch small bits of ice, fruit, or vegetables.

13 MEASURING CUP

It's essential if you want to measure out your ingredients in the right amounts. Older bars prefer to work freehand and without a measuring cup, the known as "free pouring."

14 CRUSHED ICE PUCK

It's in constant use in the USA. A few quick blows can crush ice cubes in seconds. Highly recommended for bars that don't have a crushed ice machine.

15 ICE PICK

One of the most important tools at our bar. Its main job is to chip ice off the block and shape it.

16 LARGE ICE KNIFE / BAR KNIFE

Gives the ice a clear, clean edge. We use it to split a pre-sawed ice block into smaller pieces. The details are handled by the ice pick (see above).

17 BUNSEN BURNER

A must-have for every bartender, used to char or even smoke different woods, fruits, and vegetables.

ELECTRIC MIXER (BLENDER)

An 82-year-old bartender from Sacramento once told me I should tell every guest, "The machine is broken," because any cocktail made with the machine simply wouldn't work. But if you really have to use one, it should either be the classic Hamilton Beach or a mixer from Bar Boss. These two blenders last the longest and have enough power to make several cocktails at once.

MUDDLER

For sustainability reasons, you should skip plastic here. The muddler in a bar is kind of like the mortar in a kitchen—it's used to crush or mash fruits, vegetables, herbs, and spices in the shaker.

BOTTLE OPENER AND CORKSCREW

Everyone has their favorite here. Simple, standard products are totally fine for everyday use. But if you want to play in the big leagues here too, you should check out the Laguiole brand. Because, every bartender is happy to get a great bottle opener as a gift.

"If you want to train precision and speed at a high level and give your guests the best possible quality, you also have to work with the best possible equipment."

CHOPPING BOARD

Wood is definitely the best material here, even if it means weekly care and oiling. If you've got the budget, we recommend a custom-made board for your workstation—after all, a perfectly fitted chopping board means you lose less workspace. Keep your hands off cheap stuff made from glued-together chipboard. A good chopping board costs a bit, but it'll last a long time if you treat it right.

SQUEEZE BOTTLES

There are different sizes available, and you should pick them based on how often you'll use them. They're also great for bitters and liqueurs, as well as juices and purees. It's best to try out different sizes and match them to your ingredient list and workstation.

NUTMEG GRATER

A classic spice grater is totally fine here. You can use it to grate star anise, cinnamon, tonka beans, and other spices at the bar for cocktails.

ICE SCOOP

You should never touch ice with your bare hands. That's why, of course, you use an ice scoop.

We recommend a polished scoop because it's easier to handle the ice with it. There are different sizes available here too. A smaller scoop is fine for the bar counter or at home, but if you're running an ice machine, go for a bigger one.

These tools elevate your workbench to pro level and allow you to prepare drinks in even more ways:
1. Bar spoon, 2. Cobbler shaker, 3. Mixing glass,
4. Measuring cup (jigger), 5. Bar strainer
6. Bar knife, 7. Citrus press, 8. Ice saw,
9. Swizzle stick, 10. Zester, 11. Bar tongs,
12. Double strainer, 13. Double-sided jigger,
14. Ice puck, 15. Ice pick, 16. Ice knife,
17. Bunsen burner

Techniques at the Bar

Shaking, throwing, stirring, layering, muddling, and so on these are just some of the techniques used at the bar. In this chapter, we'll walk you through the steps you need to make the best drinks and cocktails. Take your time and read through each point carefully to get the best results.

SHAKING

We prefer the vertical style of shaking cocktails. The advantage is that the shaker doesn't point at the guest, it's easier to grab, and you can mix more efficiently. Use both hands for this, and hold the bottom of the shaker in your palm. To keep a steady stance, we recommend raising your shoulders slightly and keeping your legs stable. Here, you'll use two-piece shakers—either the Boston shaker with the glass part or the Tin Tin shaker (both on page 225) with two metal parts in different sizes. It's important to always seal the shaker airtight, but be careful not to press too hard! After shaking, it can take a lot of strength to open the shaker again. It's also key to shake the shaker vertically and firmly, so the ice doesn't hit the bottom and break, but instead spins around inside. Practice makes perfect!

MEASURING/JIGGERING

Hold the jigger between your index and middle finger and keep it over the shaker. Pour in the ingredients, and once you hit the right amount, flip the jigger so the liquid flows into the shaker. One hand lifts the bottle, the other holds the jigger. Please note that so-called "free pouring"—working without a jigger—should only be used in bars with a high turnover, so-called "high volume" bars.

THROWING

Throwing a cocktail is an old-school bartending method from back when bartenders didn't have all the tools we have today. When done right, this technique can look very acrobatic and really wow the crowd and your guests. That shouldn't be your main goal, but it's a nice bonus. For throwing, you use two metal shaker parts—a big one and a small one. The bigger part with the cocktail is held just above

"Precision, practice, and more practice are the most important things to master certain bar techniques. No one should expect beginners to master the bar overnight and get everything right from the start."

the head, and the empty metal part is held just below it. Now pour in, pulling the shorter shaker down so you get a stream. Then pour the cocktail from the small shaker back into the big one and repeat the process. With this method, a kind of blend of shaking and stirring, six or seven rounds should be enough to get the mix you want. Practice makes perfect here too!

The cocktail is floated with absinthe and a sugar cube.

MUDDLING

The most common cocktail in this context is probably the *Caipirinha*, which is how the muddler became well-known here too. Using the wrong technique can give you blisters on your hands hands, and other injuries, too. You can avoid this by always cutting the fruit into small pieces before muddling them. Berries are easier to muddle and don't really need to be chopped up. When muddling, the pressing motion should be more like a twisting movement, not just full-on pressure on the fruit or whatever you're muddling.

STIRRING

Stirring is a technique you have to learn, just like all the others. Hold the mixing glass at the bottom with two fingers, and use your other hand to grab the bar spoon you'll be stirring with. The spoon should reach all the way to the bottom of the mixing glass, and the ice should be stirred clockwise. Keep stirring until you get the dilution you want and the cocktail is at the right temperature. Usually, 30 stirs are enough, so about 15 seconds. Cocktails with juices and syrups shouldn't be stirred—this technique is mostly used for short drinks or when you want to make a quick one.

STRAINING

A cocktail from the shaker always needs to be strained into the glass you want. Back in the day, people used the other half of the shaker, but a bar strainer makes this job far easier and helps you pour the drink cleanly into the glass.

LAYERING

Layering is a method that's hardly ever used anymore. A few cocktails, like the *White Russian*, are still layered by pouring cream on top of the drink. Or the almost universally known *B-52 shot*. Three ingredients are layered in a shot glass, always starting with the heaviest liquid. The one with the most sugar usually goes on the bottom, then it's covered by the lighter ingredients. To keep the layers separate, use the back of a bar spoon: before pouring the next liquid in, hold the spoon over the surface of the previous syrup, liqueur, or alcohol. A steady hand helps here, and it's also good to use the technique of pouring along the edge of the glass.

"It's important to really master the basics first, so you can build up to the trickier moves later. At first, you might want to get inspired by other bartenders, but at some point, everyone should find their own style and stick with it."

The Hawthorne strainer (see page 227) is the best tool for this. Put it into the shaker with the strainer side down and press it against the edge. Once you get the hang of it, you can lift the shaker with one hand and hold the strainer with your fingers, or use your other hand to grab the bottom of the shaker. Then pour carefully, making sure the strainer stays tight against the shaker so no ice or other bits end up in the glass

DOUBLE STRAINING

If you're dealing with herbs, spices, fruit, or berries, using a Hawthorne strainer alone isn't enough—you'll need to double strain. Double straining is also great for catching little ice chips that could spoil the drinking experience. Usually, a simple tea strainer from a specialty store does the trick and is very easy to use: Hold the strainer over the cocktail glass with one hand, and pour from the shaker (with the Hawthorne strainer in place) with the other. If it's taking too long, you can speed things up by gently tapping the edge of the tea strainer.

POURING

In my opinion, every bottle at the bar needs a pourer—it makes pouring into shakers, glasses, or jiggers far faster. This method is also cleaner, and with the right handling, you can even practice some flashy moves—though that shouldn't be your main focus. The pourer should fit tightly on the bottle neck so it doesn't slip or come off while you're pouring. Now, grab the bottle by the neck with your fingers and hold it upright. After pouring, slowly bring the bottle back to its starting position so no more liquid comes out. With practice, you can do this one-handed, but at first you'll need both hands. The famous "London cut" among bartenders takes years of practice: you pull the bottle up while pouring, stop the pour with a gentle downward motion, and then pull the bottle away in a circular movement.

> *The Japanese hard shake is a way to shake a cocktail without watering it down. That's because the ice is rotated around the inside of the shaker so that it does not break. It took me almost four years to master this art, but it was totally worth it. Kazuo Uyeda from the Tender Bar in Tokyo invented the technique.*

A cocktail is poured into a coupe using the double-strain method.

Service

BAR ADDRESSES

Germany

BERLIN

AMANO BAR
Auguststrasse 43, 10119 Berlin
amanogroup.de/en/hotels/hotel-amano/

BAR IMMERTREU
Christburgerstrasse 6, 10405 Berlin
bar-immertreu.de

BECKETTS KOPF
Pappelallee 64, 10437 Berlin
becketts-kopf.de

BUCK & BRECK
Brunnenstrasse 177, 10119 Berlin
buckandbreck.com

FRANKFURT

BARHUNDERT
Stiftstraße 34, 60313 Frankfurt a. M.
barhundert.de

SEVEN SWANS & THE TINY CUP
Mainkai 4, 60311 Frankfurt a. M.
sevenswans.de/seven-swans-and-the-tiny-cup

YALDY
Moselstraße 15, 60329 Frankfurt am Main
yaldy.bar

THE PARLOUR
Zwingergasse 6, 60313 Frankfurt a. M.
theparlour.de

HAMBURG

BAR DACAIO AT THE GEORGE HOTEL
Barcastrasse 3, 22087 Hamburg
thegeorge-hotel.de/hamburg/dacaio-bar-hamburg-alster/dacaio-bar-st-georg.php

NICK & NORA
Mühlenkamp 42, 22303 Hamburg
nickandnora.de

LE LION – BAR DE PARIS
Rathausstrasse 3, 20095 Hamburg
lelion.net

THE BOILERMAN BAR
Eppendorfer Weg 211, 20253 Hamburg
boilerman.de

COLOGNE

AL-SALAM
Eifelpl. 4, 50677 Cologne
al-salam.de

LITTLE LINK
Maastrichter Strasse 20, 50672 Cologne
littlelink.de

SHEPHEARD
Rathenauplatz 5, 50674 Cologne
shepheard.de

SPIRITS
Engelbertstrasse 63, 50674 Cologne
spiritsbar.de

MUNICH

BAR TABACCO
Hartmannstrasse 8, 80333 Munich
bartabacco.com

EL TATO
Buttermelcherstraße 9, 80469 Munich
el-tato.bar

SCHUMANN'S BAR AT THE HOFGARTEN
Odeonsplatz 6-7 1, 80539 Munich
schumanns.de

ZEPHYR BAR
Baaderstrasse 68, 80469 Munich
zephyr-bar.de

Austria

VIENNA

DINO'S AMERICAN BAR
Salzgries 19, 1010 Vienna
dinos.at

LOOS BAR
Kärntner Durchgang, 1010 Vienna
loosbar.at

THE SIGN
Liechtensteinstrasse 104–106, 1090 Vienna
thesignlounge.at

DOOR 7
Buchfeldgasse 7, 1080 Vienna
tuer7.at

Switzerland

ZURICH

OLD CROW
Schwanengasse 4, 8001 Zurich
oldcrow.ch

KRONENHALLE
Rämistrasse 4, 8001 Zurich
kronenhalle.ch

RIVE GAUCHE AT BAUR AU LAC HOTEL
Talstrasse 1, 8001 Zurich
bauraulac.ch

WIDDER BAR
Widdergasse 6, 8001 Zurich, Switzerland
widderhotel.com/essen-trinken/widder-garage/

Argentina

BUENOS AIRES

FLORERIA ATLANTICO
Arroyo 872, C1007AAB Buenos Aires
floreriaatlantico.com.ar

DOPPELGÄNGER
Av. Juan de Garay 500, Buenos Aires
doppelganger.com.ar

THE HARRISON SPEAKEASY
Malabia 1764, C1414BGQ Buenos Aires
nicky-harrison.com

VERNE CLUB
Av. Medrano 1475, Buenos Aires
vernecocktailclub.com

Australia

SYDNEY

BULLETIN PLACE
10–14 Bulletin Pl, Sydney NSW 2000
bulletinplace.com

LOBO PLANTATION
1/209 Clarence St, Sydney NSW 2000
thelobo.com.au

THE BAXTER INN
152–156 Clarence St, Sydney NSW 2000
thebaxterinn.com

THIS MUST BE THE PLACE
239 Oxford St, Darlinghurst NSW 2010
tmbtp.com.au

France

PARIS

CANDELARIA
52 Rue de Saintonge, 75003 Paris
quixotic-projects.com/venue/candelaria

DANICO
6 Rue Vivienne, 75002 Paris

LITTLE RED DOOR
60 Rue Charlot, 75003 Paris
lrdparis.com

MABEL
58 Rue d'Aboukir, 75002 Paris
mabelparis.com

Great Britain

LONDON

BAR SWIFT
2 Old Compton St, Soho, London W1D 4TQ

BAR TERMINI
7 Old Compton St, Soho, London W1D 5JE
bar-termini.com

CONNAUGHT BAR
Connaught, Carlos Pl, London W1K 2AL
the-connaught.co.uk/mayfair-bars/connaught-bar/

TAYĒR + ELEMENTARY
152 Old St, London EC1V 9BW
tayer-elementary.com

China

HONG KONG

FOXGLOVE
Printing House, 2/F, 6 Duddell St, Central, Hong Kong
foxglovehk.com

LOBSTER BAR AT THE ISLAND SHANGRI-LA
Island Shangri-La, Hong Kong, Supreme Court Road, Level 6, Pacific Place, Central, Hong Kong
shangri-la.com/hongkong/islandshangrila/dining/restaurants/lobster-bar-grill/

QUINARY
56–58 Hollywood Rd, Central, Hong Kong
quinary.hk

STOCKTON
32 Wyndham St, Central, Hong Kong
stockton.com.hk

Japan

TOKYO

BAR ORCHARD

GEN YAMAMOTO

genyamamoto.jp

TENDER BAR

STAR BAR

starbar.jp

Since all the bars in Tokyo are really hard to find and the addresses are sometimes wrong, we prefer not to list any addresses here. Instead, we recommend asking the hotel concierge or someone who speaks and reads Japanese when you're there.

Czech Republic

PRAGUE

BLACK ANGELS
Staroměstské nám. 29, 110 00 Prague 1 –
Staré Město
blackangelsbar.cz

BUGSY'S BAR
Pařížská 1068/10, Staré Město,
110 00 Prague 1 – Staré Město
bugsysbar.com

HEMINGWAY BAR
Karoliny Světlé 279/26,
110 00 Prague 1 – Staré Město
hemingwaybar.cz/bar-prague/

L'FLEUR BAR
V Kolkovně 920/5,
110 00 Prague 1 – Staré Město
lfleur.cz

USA

NEW YORK

EMPLOYEES ONLY
510 Hudson St, New York, NY 10014
employeesonlynyc.com

MAISON PREMIERE
298 Bedford Ave, Brooklyn, NY 11211
maisonpremiere.com

PDT
113 St Marks Pl, New York, NY 10009
pdtnyc.com

THE DEAD RABBIT GROCERY AND GROG
30 Water St, New York, NY 10004
deadrabbitnyc.com

SOURCES

Bar Equipment

You can find the best work tools on these sites:
bar tools and, on some sites, kitchen tools too.
Great value for money.
barfish.de
cocktailian.de
cocktailkingdom.com
intergastro.de
sokichi.vo.shopserve.jp
uberbartools.com
urbanbar.com

Spirits

Here you'll find a huge selection of top spirits
at the best prices. Even rare spirits can often be
found at these places.
bardealer.de
drinkology.de
weinquelle.com

READING RECOMMENDATIONS

Abou-Ganim, Tony, *The Modern Mixologist,*
Surrey, Chicago 2010

Baker, Charles H., *The Gentleman's Companion,*
Derrydale, New York 1939

Bar La Florida Cocktails, Lloret, Havana 1933

Bergeron, Victor Jules, *Trader Vic's Bartender's
Guide,* Doubleday, Garden City (NY) 1947

Boothby, William, *The World's Drinks and How
to Mix Them,* Boothby's World Drinks Co.,
SanFrancisco 1908/1930

Broom, Dave, *The Connoisseur's Book of Spirits
& Cocktails,* Carlton Books, Italy 1998. (The
Big Book of Spirits & Cocktails, Lichtenberg,
Munich, 2000)

Bullock, Tom, *The Ideal Bartender,* Buxton &
Skinner Printing & Stationery Company, St.
Louis 1917

Craddock, Harry, *The Savoy Cocktail Book,*
Constable & Co., London 1930

DeGroff, Dale, *The Craft of the Cocktail,*
Clarkson Potter, New York 2002

Difford, Simon, *Diffords Guide to Cocktails #7,*
Sauce Guides Limited, London 2008

Embury, David, *The Fine Art of Mixing Drinks,*
Doubleday, Garden City (NY)
1948/1952/1958

Haigh, Ted, *Vintage Spirits and Forgotten
Cocktails,* Rockport, Gloucester (MA)
2004/2009

Hess, Robert, *The Essential Bartender's Guide,*
Mud Puddle Books, New York 2008

Jackson, Michael, *Whisky,* Dorling Kindersley,
New York 2005. (Whisky.
All brands and distilleries of the world, Dorling
Kindersley, London 2005)

Johnson, Harry, *Bartenders' Manual,* self-
published, New York 1882/1888/1900

Kappeler, George J., *Modern American
Drinks,* The Merriam Company, New York 1895

MacElhone, Harry, *Harry's ABC of Mixing
Cocktails,* Odhams Press, London 1922

Masson, Jeff and Greg Boehm, *The Big Bartender's Book,* Mud Puddle Books, New York 2009

Meier, Frank, *The Artistry of Mixing Drinks,* Fryam Press, Paris 1936

Miller, Anistatia and Jared Brown, *Spirituous Journey: A History of Drink, Book Two: From Publicans to Master Mixologists,* Mixellany Ltd., London 2009

Regan, Gary, *The Joy of Mixology,* Clarkson Potter, New York 2003

Schumann, Charles, *American Bar,* Abbeville Press, New York 1995. (*American Bar,* Collection Rolf Heyne, Munich 2001)

Schumann, Charles, *Tropical Bar Book,* Stewart, Tabori & Chang, New York 1989. (*Schumann's Tropical Bar Book. Drinks and Stories,* Collection Rolf Heyne, Munich 1986)

Sloppy Joe's Cocktails Manual, self-published, Havana 1932

Tarling, William J., *Café Royal Cocktail Book,* Pall Mall Ltd., London 1937

Thomas, Jerry, *The Bar-Tender's Guide,* Dick & Fitzgerald, New York 1876/1887

Thomas, Jerry, *How to Mix Drinks,* Dick & Fitzgerald, New York 1862

Uyeda, Kazuo, *Cocktail Techniques,* Mud Puddle Books, New York 2010

INDEX

Imprint

CALLWEY 1884

© 2026 Callwey GmbH
Klenzestraße 36, 80469 Munich
buch@callwey.de
Tel.: +49 89-89 05 080-0
www.callwey.de

Catch us on Instagram:
www.instagram.com/callwey

ISBN 978-3-7667-2872-2
1st edition 2026

Bibliographic info from the German National
Library: The German National Library lists this
publication in the German National Bibliography;
detailed bibliographic data is available online at dnb.
dnb.de.

The Author

Cihan Anadologlu is a renowned bartender
and consultant for the food industry, working
internationally. After stints in major cities like New
York, London, and Hong Kong, he took on the role
of head bartender in some of the world's best bars. In
2016, he opened his own bar, "CIRCLE BY CIHAN
ANADOLOGLU" at the "Hearthouse" in Munich,
which was immediately listed among the best bars.
Anadologlu's cocktail creations have won awards
all over the world and are served at events like the
Oscars (2014), the GQ Awards, and the Bambi
Awards.

Behind the scenes

It's so exciting to publish the cocktail book of one
of the world's best bartenders! We're extremely
proud that we persuaded Cihan to share his cocktail
creations for the first time and reveal long-kept
recipe secrets! The spectagular staging of these and
Florian Gurster's delicious food is all thanks to our
photographer Daniel Esswein's passion for perfect
lighting. Spot on!

We hope you enjoy this book!

Project lead: Anna Seidel
Translation: Callwey Editorial Team
Translation editing: Alison Moffat-McLynn
Recipes: Florian Gürster, www.floundco.de
Photography: Daniel Esswein, www.danielesswein.
com; except for page 10 & 63: T. Lehmann, page 11:
M. Gnoinski & T. Menzl, page 13: akg-images, page
14: akg-images/Imagno/Austrian Archives (S)
Cover and portrait illustrations: Jörn Kaspuhl, Hamburg
Production: Oliver Meier, Isabelle Müller